Selected Writings
of John Darcy Noble

Selected Writings
of John Darcy Noble

FAVORITE ARTICLES
FROM DOLLS MAGAZINE: 1982-1995

Photographs by Lynton Gardiner

Portfolio Press

For Dorothy Dixon and Winnie Langley,
dear friends whose kindness and generosity
have so enriched my life

First Edition/First Printing

To purchase additional copies of this book, contact Portfolio Press,

130 Wineow Street, Cumberland, MD 21502; 877-737-1200.

Library of Congress Catalog Card Number 99-75061

ISBN 0-942620-26-7

Designed by John Vanden-Heuvel Design

Printed and bound by The Bath Press, Bath, England

CONTENTS

Preface

It is with great personal pride and satisfaction that I begin this preface, for this is a book that I have dreamed of for so long—a book, happily, with the publisher and especially with the editor of my choice.

It all began in the very early 1980s, when I was still the curator of the prestigious Toy Collection at the Museum of the City of New York. I had already held that position for nearly twenty years. Through my lecturing schedule, my books and especially through my very lively exhibition program, both the Toy Collection and its curator had become celebrated, I am happy to claim, throughout the toy-collecting world.

It was at the champagne opening of my big winter show—a blockbuster of an affair—that I first set eyes on a diminutive creature, whom I at once decided must be a faerie. She had wafted, I thought, or even flown, by mistake into my party. A tiny, tiny girl it was, graceful and elegant, who regarded me with huge, shining eyes and an adorable smile. "You don't know me," she said, "but I'm Krystyna Goddu, and I want to talk to you."

"How flattering of you!" I said, thinking that this was certainly a faerie name, "but it's so crowded and noisy here—could we perhaps meet some other day?"

"It's urgent!" she said.

Well, it's hard to resist a faerie. Only a few minutes later we were sitting, with our champagne, in my blessedly quiet, fuchsia-colored office, accompanied by a quiet, dark-haired gentleman called Robert Rowe. Robert, it transpired, had just established a brand-new doll magazine, to be called, not surprisingly, *Dolls*. Krystyna was the editor, and would I consent to become a regular feature writer?

I was even more flattered. We arrived at terms to our mutual satisfaction, and within a few months the first issue of *Dolls* was published, with my first leading story.

And this really is a faerie-tale, for *Dolls* magazine blossomed, and so did my friendship with Krystyna. She came to understand, perhaps more than anyone, the pivotally important role that my love of old toys has played, for all my long life, in the direction taken by my scholarship and in the evolution of my philosophy. Her support and encouragement have always been there, and were especially precious through all the trials and readjustments of retirement.

I have never, alas, had children of my own, although I believe that I would have been very good at parenthood. Instead, I had accumulated, over the years, a family of grown-up god-children, who are the next best thing. When Krystyna heard of this, she said, "So, why can't I be your god-daughter, too?" And so she is.

In all, over the years, there were nearly one hundred of my articles published in *Dolls* magazine. The selection here includes some of my very favorites. I hope this book will be a great success, so that it may be followed, in due course, by another—and another.

For the truth is, I have missed working with my tiny, tiny faerie god-daughter. I am simply delighted that we can be together again.

John Darcy

John Darcy Noble

Introduction

by Krystyna Poray Goddu
Founding editor, *Dolls* Magazine

One of the greatest and most lasting gifts I received in the many years I edited *Dolls* magazine was my friendship with John Darcy Noble. It was immediately a friendship, for John is surely incapable of having such a thing as a "purely professional" relationship. His profession was, and remains, integral to his life, and to enter into a professional relationship with him is to enter into his rich and varied life.

Our goal in publishing *Dolls* magazine was, from the start, to bring to the subject of doll collecting the level of quality in writing, photography and graphics that we believed the subject deserved. In pursuit of that goal, I discouraged first-person writing in the magazine, recognizing that too much of what had been written about dolls had been first-person sentimentality and nostalgia. In our effort to bring a professional level of reportage and scholarship to the magazine, we edited the stories we received into informative, impersonal pieces of journalism. But as soon as I received John's first article, "Behind the Scenes: The Making of a Museum Exhibition," which appeared in our premiere issue, I understood that I had to make an exception to my rule. The personal tone of John's writing makes for its very richness. He brings to his great love of dolls his scholarship, his artistic talent and training, his lifelong experience with antique toys and his inimitable style—in short, himself. There are certain writers we read regardless of their subject, because we are eager to know what they have to say about any-thing. John is one of those writers.

Still, I believe his subjects were always of great interest to our readers, whether he told the intimate story of how a museum exhibit comes to be; gave a fascinating history lesson in the development of the renowned Italian Lenci company; or reflected on his own beloved pieces, those in museums he knew well, or those of his friends, such as the legendary collectors Dorothy Dixon and Winnie Langley. Rereading these articles in preparation for selection, I was enveloped by their aura all over again. I remembered the long telephone conversations with John that preceded every assignment, for he had to present the marvels of each story to me before I received it in writing.

In editing *Dolls* magazine, I thought of myself as an orchestra conductor, blending a broad mix of instruments, rhythms and melodies into one rich and harmonious whole. At the same time, an editor, like a conductor, must be careful that each individual voice is pure and true to itself. And that the occasional solos soar. John's voice is one of wonder, romance and sophistication. His solos did soar, and carried his readers into his realm—what he calls the faerie realm. I call it a realm of heightened sensibility, one you enter when you are alertly open to the wonder and beauty in every experience and every object.

One of John's great talents is to imbue whatever is dear to him with a mystique that borders on the unreal—witness his enchanting preface to this book. Over the years I have read about many people, places and objects in his life, all described with his magical turns of phrase. I never expected to be the subject of his writing and now that I have been, I will never be the same again. From now on, part of me will always be the faerie that I am in John's eyes and words.

So altered, too, are the treasures that he loves and writes about. I chose to select, for this book, his writings about antiques. Forced to limit and focus the selection, I reluctantly put aside his important articles about contemporary dolls, which are filled with great insight, perspective and the same magical flair.

The 35 stories in this book were mutually selected by John and myself. Among them are many of my favorites, though many others, unavoidably, have been left out. It is hard to pick a favorite among favorites, but there are a few for which I have especially fond feelings. I share with John a great love for early wooden dolls, so I am pleased we could include "A Story of Suitable Sentiments," the tale of an 18th-century English wooden, Mary King, and "A Moppet, A Poppet, A Dainty Darlyng," about a rare 18th-century wooden baby. "Plain and Fancy Handiwork" was another article I enjoyed preparing for publication, for in it John included pages from the 19th-century *American Girl's Book*, which instructed girls in dollmaking, among other things. It was difficult to pull myself out of the era of stitchery into my late-20th-century world of computers.

Most of the very beautiful pictures in this book are by Lynton Gardiner, who has become known as the pre-eminent photographer of dolls. Lynton was on staff at The Metropolitan Museum of Art when John hired him to photograph the Toy Collection at the Museum of the City of New York. He then generously shared him with us, and Lynton's photographs, for John's articles and for many others, played a great role in creating the elegant look *Dolls* magazine became known for.

I like to believe that the stories John wrote for me at *Dolls* magazine are among the best pieces of his writing, but I need only read his 1987 introduction to the Mingei Museum's catalog for their exhibition *First Collections: Dolls and Folk Toys of the World* to know that he brings his rare mix of sense and sensibility to all his writing. In that introduction he wrote movingly about play: "It is the highly evolved artist, amongst others, who devotes himself, with religious fervor and single-mindedness, to a lifetime of play. . . in reviewing the playthings of our past in connection with those of other cultures, one is struck. . . by the expressions of the urge to play that are common, we find, to all mankind. . . . Of all the artifacts. . . those made for children are the most vivid, evoking the direct response, lifting the heart with delight or inducing the most subtle of melancholies." If he credits me here with being one who understands "perhaps more than anyone" the importance of old toys in his life, and the direction of his scholarship and philosophy, it is because I have taken much of his writing to my own heart and mind, until it has become the foundation of my own philosophy of play and playthings.

John has long been held in the highest esteem by doll scholars. In their introduction to his 1971 book, *A Treasury of Beautiful Dolls*, the respected doll authorities, Dorothy, Elizabeth and Evelyn Coleman wrote: "Thanks to the efforts of scholarly and sensitive people like John Noble, old dolls are beginning to be recognized as important historical artifacts; they reflect both the artistic modes and the social norms of the day."

Laudatory—and true—as these remarks are, they do not evoke the unique magic of John's writing, which colors his scholarship and experience. But who could evoke it? We must turn to the writing itself. Open your heart and prepare to be lifted into the marvelous realm of John Darcy Noble.

PART I
1982-1988

In the early articles, many of which were
written during the author's curatorial days,
he often shared treasures from
his museum's collection.

The Making of a Museum Exhibition

AN INSIDE LOOK AT HOW A DOLL EXHIBITION COMES TO BE—AND THE STORY OF A SURPRISING DISCOVERY MADE DURING THE PREPARATIONS FOR ONE UPCOMING SHOW

W e have been left, by an earlier generation of doll collectors, a legacy of tantalizing legends—tantalizing because, much as we long for them to be true, no factual basis for them has yet been found. One of the most alluring of these legends concerns the famous couturier, Charles Frederick Worth. It is said that a certain dolls' dressmaker of Paris held a license from the House of Worth, permitting 14 model dresses to be copied, in dolls' sizes, every year.

Charles Frederick Worth is himself a legend, an English lad, born in Lincolnshire, who arrived in Paris just before he was 20. Barely 14 years later he was famous, dressmaker to the Empress Eugenie herself. He is a fascinating figure; a genius, an innovator, an autocrat who chose his clients as carefully as he chose his friends. He created the entire mystique of French luxury—"Le Luxe"—and he invented, single-handedly, the fashion world as we know it today.

The Costume Collection of the Museum of the City of New York possesses a large number of superb Worth dresses, worn by such fabled New Yorkers as Mrs. Cornelius Vanderbilt, Mrs. J.P. Morgan and Mrs. Sandford White. They will be seen this winter in a major exhibition called The House of Worth: The Gilded Age, conceived and realized by the museum's

This close view reveals the details of the 1860s ball gown believed to have been made by Worth himself.

PHOTOS: SERGIO PENCHANSKY

two that belonged to Emma Rockefeller.

For this exhibition, the focus was to be on the dolls' costumes. Since so many of these lady dolls came with wardrobes, we decided to review the put-away dresses, many of which were ball gowns, so that as many dolls as possible could appear in clothes that have never been seen before.

Most of these dresses had been shelved for years. Jane diligently rooted out their dusty boxes, and we discov-

Left, a full-length view of the restored ball gown believed to have been made by Worth shows off the success of the restoration efforts. Below is a preview of some of the costumes being shown for the first time at the museum's exhibition. Seen in the Wintergarden, from left foreground: One of the museum's celebrated treasures, a doll with a blown-leather body and her own dress made by La Veuve Clement; a Huret doll in her own original costume; a doll wearing a dress from about 1875; center back, an early lady doll with bisque swivel head and forearms wearing a white tarlatan ball gown; a doll that once belonged to Emma Rockefeller wearing mourning clothes from her own wardrobe; right foreground, a late 1870s gown of pearl-colored faille also suspected to have been made by Worth himself.

Curator of Costumes, JoAnne Olian.

Charles Frederick Worth also designed clothes for actresses to wear on the stage—for Eleonora Duse and Ida Rubinstein—and and for American actresses too—Mary Garden and Ada Rehan among them. At the museum so many Worths were discovered among the Theatre Collection's costumes that a second show will be mounted this winter, to be called Theatrical Worth.

Like the House That Jack Built, the preparations for these two exhibitions started a chain of events that led to the discovery of a doll that may have been dressed by the House of Worth.

To begin, I decided to complement the two Worth shows with a Christmas display of French Lady dolls in the museum's beautiful entrance hall. Instead of seasonal snow and tinsel, my assistant, Jane Hirschkowitz, and I, planned a verdant winter garden, with lawns and fountains, ferns and lilies, live parrots and cockatoos. There would be shimmering light, we decided, and the dolls would dance and promenade to a consort of harps.

The Toy Collection is especially rich in Lady Dolls, and there are some celebrated rarities, including five Hurets, the glazed porcelain Rohmer and her identical sister in bisque, the Veuve Clement with her blown kid body and dolls with illustrious provenance, such as the

ered many exciting treasures. We sometimes discovered dilapidations, too—split seams, tattered laces—and it was clear that repairs, expert repairs, would be needed.

But help was at hand. The Toy Collection is lucky to have two very talented volunteers: Margaret Molnar, who was trained in textile conservation in Switzerland and Douglas James, a skillful and sensitive dollmaker. They share a great affection for these lovely old dolls, and now they cheerfully pooled their resources and

began the slow, painstaking process of restoration.

One morning I brought them a large dress box. "Here's a real challenge for you," I said. It contained the remains of a doll's ball gown of the late 1860s, a huge crinoline of ivory-colored silk and spangled tulle. It had been decorated with silver lace and garnet roses, but the tulle overskirt had crumbled entirely away, leaving all the trimmings loose—a boxful of pieces.

It belonged to a beautiful pale bisque doll, one of two that were the gift, a few years ago, of Mrs. Charles D. Webster. The doll came to us wearing an equally splendid day dress: emerald-green taffeta boldly ornamented with pearl-encrusted lace. In the bottom of the box was a third dress of violet and white silk, with a pattern of shadowy flowers, but much crumpled and discolored.

The first thing to do was to look at the dresses on "mannequins" to assess the extent of the decay. The two ladies who accompany our famous Seventh Regiment Officer dolls were the same size as Mrs. Webster's bisque, and this was felicitous, for their own dresses were too ragged to consider restoring in time for this exhibition. The Webster dresses fitted them perfectly, and this meant that all three could be shown, if

they could be restored.

Margaret thought that the violet dress was in excellent condition, and could safely be steamed and the gauze blouse and petticoat wet-cleaned. A week later the dress reappeared, fresh as the daisies in its pattern. As Jane padded the great crinoline—for there was no hoop in the collection big enough—we began to realize that these were no ordinary gowns. The violet one was brilliantly and wittily designed, and executed with a sweep of majesty that I have not seen before in doll's clothes.

It was Phyllis Magidson, Assistant Curator of Costumes, who first linked these dresses with the name of Worth. The silk tulle with its tiny, squared-off spangles was a favorite conceit of his, she told us, and the ivory silk of the underskirt was the exact fabric used by Worth for linings and for the support, as in this dress, of delicate fabrics. When the dolls' dresses were examined, the details of cut, of the stitching and finishing of seams and other constructions were all found to be the same as in the full-sized Worth gowns. A doll dressed by Worth...?

But where in the world would we find two yards of ivory silk tulle, scattered with minute, square metal spangles? Since the tulle had remained intact on the skirt flounces, the match had to be exact—no easy task.

Douglas James found the answer. A generous hem of the tulle was crushed behind the silver lace border of the

missing overskirt, and it had retained its spangles. And a search of the original box in which the dolls had lain for years, wrapped in newspapers dated before 1900, revealed whole masses of loose spangles in its corners.

A costume plate of a similar dress—certainly by Worth—showed a tulle overskirt ruched on the six seams on the skirt. "If we can match the silk tulle, I can cut and seam the overskirt, using the silk skirt as a pattern," said Douglas. "Then all I have to do is to rule out a grid, pin the tulle skirt over it, and glue the spangles into place."

He started at one side, and Margaret started at the other, and it took them only two days to glue on all the spangles. The skirts came together smoothly, as Douglas had predicted; the silver lace fell into its position above the flounces, and there were just the right number of sprays of roses to pin the overskirt on each seam.

Douglas then undertook the exacting task of replacing the tulle which had once covered the bodice and the double puffed sleeves. The little posy with the garnet velvet streamers had a backing, a wired circle of brown silk net, implying a hair ornament. Pinned in place, one streamer reached to the hem of the dress, the other to the edge of the overskirt, just as they were intended to do, while the pendant, star-shaped sequins which had puzzled us all as to their purpose, dropped into place vertically, giving an effect of great richness. Jane found hair ornaments with similar streamers depicted in fashion plates.

When the three dolls were brought together, the impact of the dresses was startling. "They really are quite unlike other dolls' clothes," I said to Phyllis Magidson. "They have a haughtiness and assurance— even arrogance..."

"Yes," she said, "Those are just the qualities that make Worth dresses so unlike any others, so recognizable."

Mrs. Webster dressed at Worth and so did her mother before her. It is known that Charles Frederick Worth liked his American customers and became great friends with some of them. He was also fond of children, and it is quite feasible that dolls' dresses were made sometimes, to surprise a favored child on her birthday—perhaps miniatures of the dresses ordered by her mother, and made up from remnants of the fabrics. Was Mrs. Webster's mother just such a lucky child?

Or perhaps there is truth in the old rumor after all, and these are, at last, examples of the dresses copied under license from Worth. But Phyllis Magidson doubts this—they have too much panache, she says, to be copies. Certainly such garments, constructed with all the flair and authority of labeled Worths, could not have been made without the couturier's knowledge.

We may never be certain, but it is endlessly fascinating to wonder. Hereafter, we at the museum will look at original lady dolls' clothes with inquiring eyes. "I wonder," said Jane, pointing to a lavish promenade dress of the 1870s, its train longer than the doll is high. The pearl-colored faille is a froth of scallops, piped in lavender. "You know, Worth loved those colors—and he actually re-invented scallops—now I wonder..."

Meanwhile, the Webster doll and her two friends can be seen during the holidays season, parading these wonderful gowns in their own Wintergarden, where they eclipse all the other dresses—and even the green parrots and the cockatoo—with their magnificence. Come and see them, won't you, and judge for yourself?

Great Names in Dollmaking: Lenci

To American collectors today the name means felt dolls, but Lenci actually encompasses an entire art movement of the early 20th century

Italy is a country with a splendid cultural heritage, and in the Italian town of Torino, there is an old factory with a cultural heritage of its very own. It is the home of Lenci, an art movement comparable to William Morris's Arts and Crafts movement in England.

The Lenci movement began in 1919, in a world with a new technology, with electricity and air travel and mass media, a world with a brave new idealism.

After every great international conflict, for a brief decade or so, this optimism appears—the belief that now the world will live in Olympian peace and plenty. It is this Arcadian dream that is the essence of the Lenci movement.

There were similar impulses in artistic circles all over the world during that era. We have named them collectively "Art Deco," a French name, for we tend to think of Art Deco as a French style. After all, at that time all high fashion, whether in dress or decor, originated in Paris.

The idea of an Italian Art Deco with a distinctive style of its own is startling at first, until we remember that other art movements have had national manifestations. Art Nouveau, for instance, originated some 20 years earlier in Paris, but English Art Nouveau, typified by the craftsmen of Liberty of London, has its own recognizable, Celtic flavor, while in Scotland the Art Nouveau movement, which centered around the astonishing Charles Rennie Macintosh, has a linear clarity and faerie lyricism unique to itself.

The Lenci movement was founded by Enrico Scavini and his wife Elena. Until recently, most of our information about its early days came from surviving catalogs, old advertisements and gossipy newspaper reports. In one of these last, it was stated that the name Lenci was a pet name for Elena. However,

"Jules" stands about 17 inches high. He appears in the 1927, 1930 and 1931 Lenci catalogs, and is shown here alongside the original design by Dudovitch.

PHOTOS: CARL NARDIELLO

the origin of the name can actually be found in the old trademark, first registered in 1919: a child's spinning top surrounded by the motto of the company: "Ludus Est Nobis Constanter Industria," which freely translates as: "To Play is our Constant Work." The initials of this motto form the word LENCI, which was adopted as the name of the company in 1922. Perhaps at that time Elena was referred to as "Madame Lenci," just as today the present owner, Beppe Garella, is often spoken of as "Mr. Lenci."

The Lenci company brought together under one roof and one name an imposing roster of young and visionary artists, including Dudovitch, Jacopi, Mario Riva and Mario Sturani, some of whom were already famous in the Italian art world. For Lenci, they produced an array of exciting merchandise for modern living.

The phenomenal, international success of the Lenci dolls—the Scavinis' first love—has obscured for us in America the diversity of the Lenci products. There was clothing for children, including imaginative fancy dress; there were deliciously frivolous hats and handbags; there was furniture, sometimes marvelously inlaid, and there were furnishings, including pillows and lampshades, wall hangings—even sewing baskets. In Italy at that time it

was possible to give a dinner party in a Lenci-decorated room, and to lay the table with cloth and napkins, centerpiece, place settings and cutlery, all from Lenci. And dazzling it would have been.

It comes as a surprise to doll-oriented Americans to discover that, in some European circles, the Lenci factory is famous not for its dolls but for its ceramics. For 35 years, Lenci's chinacraft output was enormous. Thousands of pieces were produced by its talented sculptors, and several of them—Bertetti, Vacchetti, Maraini, Ducato, Ronzan, Grande and Guigo—went on to found factories of their own, which developed and amplified the Lenci style.

The pieces were often large and sumptuous, mostly figurines, although bowls and vases were also popular. Often the subject matter was taken from classical mythology, but with so many artists there was an amazing variety, both of style and of content. However, they all shared the qualities of boldness and richness, and the aura of innocence that is associated with the Lenci movement. From 1928 onwards, Lenci's chinaware achieved artistic

"Pluci," a golfer doll offered in the current Lenci line (center), first appeared in a sketch dating from 1927 (left). He stands about 17½ inches in height; an early version of Pluci is in the photo.

stature comparable to that of its great French and Scandinavian contemporaries.

All these products were new and exciting. They sang of a world made fresh and young, a world where the sun shone and flowers bloomed and children laughed. One can only imagine the energy and creative excitement, not to mention the business acumen, that in a few short years made the Lenci name internationally known, and the Lenci products not only famous but highly fashionable.

There had of course been "art dolls" in the world before, notably the waxen costume dolls that had been the rage in Paris for a few years in the early 1900's. But not until Lenci did such art dolls become status symbols, both in the nursery and in the boudoir. Early advertisements show clearly that the dolls were intended as luxurious art objects.

"Develop artistic tendencies in your children," says an advertisement in the May 1923 issue of *Playthings* magazine. "Buy a Lenci doll to place on a hassock, to lend color to your boudoir, to decorate a corner of your limousine,"—but not, one notices, to play with. And the excellent condition of so many of the surviving Lenci dolls implies that they were not often bought to be played with. They were beautiful and expensive, and they gave to the home that cachet of taste and culture that was to be achieved in the 1950's by the display of a Picasso plate, and in the 1970's by a Lichtenstein lithograph or a Warhol soup can. By an amusing paradox, Lenci dolls have achieved that same status today. They appeal especially to young collectors—to whom the 1920's must seem like the remote past—and in many a smart New York loft or San Francisco apartment a Lenci doll is the ultimate status symbol.

The 23-inch "Dschang-go" (left) and "Butterfly" (center) dolls were sold in 1925 and 1927. "Kamimura" (right), 40 inches tall, dates from 1928.

18

This lady in Hungarian costume is 40 inches high and dates from approximately 1925.

The construction of the Lenci dolls is completely original. There had been felt dolls made elsewhere, but they had been pieced to achieve their contours, with seams down the center of their faces, and they were, almost of necessity, stylized and cartoon-like. The Lenci invention was the use of the two-part die that took advantage of the give of the material to mold the entire head in one piece. The body is also constructed from felt, with sophisticated joints that are almost invisible.

Lenci faces are quite different from other dolls, with expressions of great subtlety—some dreamy and faraway, some withdrawn and moody, some alert and even surprised. They are arrestingly lifelike. Their costumes are vividly colorful, with a use of fabric that still seems original today. In the 1920's it must have seemed most innovative with its heavy reliance on felt and organdy, its richness of pattern and texture, its hand-embroidery and intricate, felt-on-felt patchwork. The craftsmanship is superb, and the designs bold and exuberant, with little concern, it seems, for the great number of working hours that each doll must consume. It is not surprising that the finished dolls were very expensive indeed.

Today, those early dolls can command high prices on the secondary market. In 1982, a 16½-inch-high child doll dating from the very early days of the facto-

ry, circa 1920, sold for $330 at a Christie's East sale in New York. The larger portrait dolls bring much higher numbers: last year Marvin Cohen Auctions in New Lebanon, New York, sold a 25-inch-high Marlene Dietrich doll from the early 1930's for $1,100, while Sotheby Parke Bernet in New York sold a 29-inch-high Rudolph Valentino dressed as "The Sheik," circa 1929, for $4,125.

The Lenci tradition is continuous. The factory workrooms are unchanged, their walls and furniture painted in the same bright colors with which the craftspeople were always surrounded. Today's artisans are mostly the descendants of those original craftspeople, many of whom are still alive, and whose skills their progeny have inherited.

The Lenci dolls being made today are reissues of old designs in limited editions. They are made with the original equipment and methods from the 1920's. It must be emphasized that these are not reproductions, but true Lenci originals. They differ slightly from the older versions, notably in the scale of the patchwork patterns which, because they involve a great deal of finicky work, are very expensive to produce. And they have the undefinable ambiance of today—and it is good, fitting and proper that they should be, in subtle ways, distinguishable from the dolls made 50 years ago. But they are authentic Lenci dolls, and as such are highly collectible. Lenci dolls have never been ordinary, and they never will. They are among the aristocrats of the doll world, whether they were made yesterday or today.

Cataloging the dolls of the past, dating and attributing them, is usually a matter of painstaking research. In the Lenci factory, as though by a miracle, the records are all preserved, together with original designs, molds, templates and fabric swatches, as well as many wonderful specimen dolls that were kept as examples. The factory is a treasury for the historian. Beppe Garella, the present owner of Lenci, is a warm and welcoming man, proud of the Lenci heritage, and eager for it to be understood and properly valued.

The Saga of the Salem Doll

AFTER TWO DECADES OF DOUBT, THE ENIGMATIC MEHITABEL HODGES
IS RESTORED TO HER RIGHTFUL, RESPECTED STATUS

The 1920's and 1930's were the heyday of doll collecting, and it was during that time that the first legendary dolls began to appear. Their names became household words in doll-collecting circles and their pictures appeared in all the doll books of their day. Among them, Mehitabel Hodges, the 18th-century doll known as the "Salem doll," enjoyed movie-star celebrity. And yet, for the past 20 years she has receded into obscurity. She is never seen in person, and her picture is strikingly absent from the new doll books. What is the reason for this mysterious fall from grace?

Her story is perhaps a saga, which reads like a detective yarn—from the shattering of her reputation and her shameful retirement to the appearance of her champions on both sides of the Atlantic. Let us look first at her story as it appeared in print in the 1940's. A Captain Gamaliel Hodges of Salem, Massachusetts, set sail for China in 1715. In France he bought a doll for his daughter, Mehitabel, elaborately dressed in the fashion of the day. It was said that Captain Hodges did not return to Salem until 1724.

The doll, we were told, was treasured by subsequent generations of Hodges girls, who named it Mehitabel after its first owner. All this information is from family oral history, which seems to have been written down for the first time in the 1890's, when the doll was exhibited for charity. A photograph taken at the time shows the doll looking just as it does today. By the 1940's it had passed into the collection of Imogene Anderson of New York City, and was widely publicized as the first "fashion doll" ever to come to America. She became one of the most famous and most coveted of dolls.

In 1961, with loud fanfare, Mehitabel Hodges was given to the Museum of the City of New York, together with a number of other rare and famous dolls. I had just come to New York for a holiday and was hired as a con-

sultant to authenticate this important gift. It was my first contact with the museum, which was to become so central in my life. Of the dozen or so dolls that I examined then, the only one about which I had reservations was Mehitabel—but alas, they were serious ones.

First of all, there was the dismaying fact that the doll itself was of a late kind, a glass-eyed wooden of a sort made at the latter end of the 18th century, but not in 1715. And then she was dressed, in the height of fashion, certainly, but it was the fashion of the late 1770's or early 1780's, and a startling one for her to have worn in 1724!

An authority on costuming, who shall be nameless, condemned this dress out of hand. "Weighted silk!" she said. "From the 1890's probably. And the pink color is a coal-tar dye, also from the late 19th century—look where it has faded; 18th-century silk never fades like that. And look at this machine-made lace! This dress was made in the 1890's. There was a big revival of interest in the 18th century then, you know."

I did know, and I also knew that this costume, with its finicky stitching and pretty, fussy trimmings, was quite unlike the coarsely sewn, boldly trimmed clothing worn by other 18th-century dolls. The only answer that I could find to these riddles was that the doll had been rediscovered—in a family attic perhaps—in the 1890's and had been redressed at that time, and that amateur research into the doll's family history had exaggerated the details of the doll's origin.

It was the only likely answer, but the riddles remained, and they were depressing ones for the museum. Mehitabel had become an embarrassment, not an ornament, to the Toy Collection. A redressed doll is usually worthless to a museum, and with her dubious history to boot, poor Mehitabel was discredited. I was instructed to remove her from exhibition as soon as possible. She stood forlornly in a dark cupboard, like a wrong hushed up, for over 20 years, deliberately forgotten.

Mehitabel Hodges, her reputation cleared, poses in her original 18th-century, fine Italian silk dress.

Dorothy Coleman was her first rescuer. Ten years after the "Salem doll's" retirement, Dorothy became interested and puzzled by the discrepancies in the story. As a professional researcher, her first action was to check out the genealogy of the Hodges family of Salem, Massachusetts.

Her findings were spectacular. There was indeed a Gamaliel Hodges in the late 18th century, but he was a cooper by profession. But there was a Benjamin Hodges, who was born in 1754 and died in 1806, who was one of the most famous sea captains to sail out of Salem harbor. There was also a Gamaliel Hodges born 1766 (died 1850) who was a sea captain and successful merchant. Either of these two sailors could have brought home the late-18th-century wooden doll.

The doll came with a wallpaper-covered bandbox from the Federal period, and she was wrapped in a silk handkerchief of the same date. By tradition, these have always belonged to her. In one corner of the handkerchief are the initials "H.H." in fine cross-stitch embroidery.

Benjamin Hodges had a daughter called Hannah (baptized in 1794) and, although both sea captains had other daughters, it is tempting to think that in Hannah we have found the original owner of the doll. We can also begin to understand the confusion that occurred when Mehitabel's history was first researched in the 1890's.

"It often happens in family histories," said Dorothy. "Names are handed down, causing confusion, as in this family, and dates on old, indistinct documents are misread, optimistically, by descendant researchers, wanting in their hearts for things to be older. But whichever of these two sea captions brought back the doll Mehitabel, it was clearly done in the early 19th century, not the 18th."

Dorothy had found the doll's origin and perhaps its first owner, but the embarrassment of the dress remained. Now I accused the 1890 Hodges ladies of redressing their doll in a style 50 years too early, based on their inaccurate dating. And Mehitabel returned to her cupboard.

It was not until another decade had passed that she found her second champion. He was David Walker, the brilliant English stage designer, who is an expert on 18th-century costume. David is an old friend who takes passionate interest in the dolls and toys and ephemera that come and go in my life.

He pounced on Mehitabel. "Now that is a wonderful dress! Look at the tiebacks on the skirt! Look at the tight sleeves, the triple cuffs and double ruffles! Those were such fleeting fashions—how wonderful to see them preserved!"

"The dress is real, then? It's not a 19th-century reproduction?"

"Oh heavens, no! They would never have understood the subtleties and elegance of this dress. The wig, too, is exactly right, with its crescent-shaped pad of tow over which the hair is raised, and so is the cap, with its spangled ribbons. There's no other way you could see this hairstyle in real life."

"But what about the weighted silk?" I asked. "The Victorian coal-tar dye? The machine-made trimmings?"

"Whoever suggested such things? I know my silks, and this is not weighted. This is fine 'Italian' silk, the kind you often find on 18th-century creche figures. And pink dyes are notoriously fugitive, in any age. As for the trimming, it is expensive, hand-knotted silk lace!"

"So this is a real 18th-century dress?"

"Oh, without question. And it was made by a professional dressmaker, with great skill and care. It was never put together with a child in mind."

Once pointed out, all this was embarrassingly obvious. But the dress had been condemned by an "expert" when I had less knowledge than I have now. I had meekly accepted her judgement, and while Mehitabel had been out of sight, I had no occasion to revise it.

David suggested that Mehitabel had been dressed, in the late 1770's, as a kind of fashion doll, rather than a child's toy, but not one of the mythical "traveling fashion dolls" that were taken about the countryside to display the latest fashions. Neither of us has ever seen one of those and until I do, my opinion is that they were full-sized or half-sized mannequins. The clothes would have been made to take off and would have been accompanied by toiles, muslin patterns of clothes that could be copied.

But Mehitabel's stylish dress is sewn in place, and she is in any case too small, and her figure too crudely stylized, to be used as a mannequin. She is set up more as a display piece than as a demonstration of fashion. I believe that she was just that: a doll dressed to catch the eye in the window of a milliner's shop or toy shop—the 18th-century equivalent of today's boutique. The doll would have demonstrated to the passers-by the taste and skills of the establishment.

How do I think she got to Salem, Massachusetts? I suspect that the shop she was in must have been in or near a seaport where the captain's ship paused on its journey—and I would think Plymouth or Portsmouth in England more likely than France, considering the times. Her dress would have gone out of fashion quickly, and then she would have been sold off as a child's plaything, and passed from one generation to another. By 1815 or thereabouts, she could well have found her way to a second-hand shop, the kind that, in seaports, bought the curios that sailors brought home from abroad. Such shops still existed, in Portsmouth, as late as the 1950's. I think that the captain bought a quaint old doll for his daughter, but one still grand enough to ensure her being the focus of great interest in Salem, both at the time and for generations to come.

After 20 years of doubt, Mehitabel's reputation was cleared, although there still remained the minor inaccuracy of her name. None of the Hodges girls was called Mehitabel, not even the original, incorrect Gamaliel's daughter.

Once again, Dorothy came to Mehitabel's rescue. Researching further, she found a second family of Hodges (the "Taunton" branch), none of whom ever went to sea. There was a Mehitabel in every generation. New England families were close enough for the two girls to know each other, and what is more likely than that Hannah should have named her doll for her best friend?

So there stands Mehitabel Hodges, out of her cupboard and happy at last. She is truly a late-18th-century "fashion doll" with an interesting family history. Her 1890 biographers were guilty of no more than well-intentioned, but amateur, research. As her admirers have always claimed, she is almost certainly the first such fashion doll to arrive in America. And it doesn't matter in the least that she made the journey when she was 50 years old!

Plain and Fancy:
A Historical Celebration of China Dolls

THESE DOLLS TYPIFY THE 19TH CENTURY BUT, PARADOXICALLY,
LITTLE IS KNOWN ABOUT THEM TODAY

Fashion is a fickle business. There are fashions in everything, from philosophy to philately, from architecture to earrings. There are, of course, fashions in doll collecting, and they come and go: the Cinderellas of today are the celebrities of tomorrow.

Until very recently, the old china dolls were Cinderellas, languishing unloved and unwanted. And yet, of all the bewildering variety of dolls made for children in the 19th century, perhaps the most common and most popular were these dolls with molded china heads (and sometimes arms and legs), which were exported in great quantities from Germany all over the world.

These dolls typify the toys of the 19th century, just as the classic wooden dolls typify the 18th, and it is a paradox that, like their wooden sisters, the china dolls are mysteries. Facts about them are few, although misinformation abounds. But the dolls themselves are numerous and, while the simple ones are very common, there is also a dazzling variety of rare models to choose from. However much we think we know, and however many we have seen, new and different examples appear all the time.

The earliest seem to date from the 1840's, that curious decade, so quiet and demure after the alarms and excursions of the first years of the century. Queen Victoria of England was crowned in 1837 and married in 1840, and her domestic bliss sums up this gentle decade. The 1840's were the peak of the Romantic period, just before the influx of materialism that followed the industrial explosion which, by mid-

century, had changed the world forever.

These moods and changes are clearly reflected in the china dolls and are part of their fascination. The first ones were very expensive toys, products of a few great porcelain factories. They are almost exclusively German, although a few tantalizing beauties were made at the Royal Copenhagen Works in Denmark.

It is extraordinary that so little should be known about artifacts that were produced in millions for more than 60 years. Current research is beginning to compare and match individual dolls, and recognizable

manufacturers are emerging, but most of these remain anonymous. A few rare dolls have been discovered with the Meissen mark, but their dates are questionable and, while one or two have been placed, optimistically, in the 18th century, most would seem to have been made much later, coinciding stylistically with the pincushion dolls of the 1920's.

Among the earliest and best of the marked dolls are the ones from the Royal Berlin factory, whose mark bears the initials K.P.M. for Konigliche Porzellan Manufactur. Their dolls are distinguished by the richness of their glaze, and by the serious, sensitive modeling of their faces. They have a wistful, almost melancholy air, and there are many women with restrained, elegant coiffures, a few rare and beautiful men and a surprising number of handsome boys, with the characteristic side part and windswept locks. These very early chinas set a standard of excellence.

A group of early chinas is shown in **illustration 1**. They are not marked, but together form a summary of the characteristics of the period. All of them have brown hair. The lady in the left foreground is calm and serene, with a classic neck and deep, sloping shoulders. Her hair is in the style worn by the young Queen Victoria at the time of her coronation and universally identified with her. China dolls that wear this coiffure were—and sometimes are still—lauded by

collectors as portraits of Queen Victoria. But this style was worn at the time by women all over Europe, and the attribution is most improbable.

The charming boy in this group came with his name: "Yankee Tom," and his blue woolen jacket with white duck trousers do indeed suggest New England and the sea. His brown hair is so dark as to be almost black, and his features are very simply and directly painted. As with many of these early dolls, the freedom and vitality of the paintings suggests the work of a very skilled porcelain craftsman who had not previously painted many doll heads, unlike the very slick painting of the later dolls.

The large lady in the green dress has often, in the past, been mistakenly called "Jenny Lind," as though she were meant to be a portrait. The connection with the singer is there, although it has nothing to do with the doll. It concerns only her dress. The lady who was preparing the doll as a present went to

Jenny Lind's historic concert in New York's Castle Garden, in 1851. Like most of the audience, she was overwhelmed by the grace and charm of the singer, and entranced by the purity of her voice. Her euphoria lasted until the next day, when she decided to dress the doll in a copy of the green dress worn by Jenny Lind. She found the fabric store mobbed by excited ladies, while the distracted clerks cut off dress lengths, as fast as they could, from silk and wool gauze in the color already known as "Jenny Lind Green." By the time she reached the counter, the fabric was sold out, although it was still available in "scarf width," wide enough for the doll's dress.

This large and extremely beautiful head is unusual in that the knot of hair at the nape is missing—the head was glazed and fired without it. Too odd to be intentional, this must have been a factory oversight, and adds distinction to a doll already rare and desirable.

The man in this group is the most unusual, and his round, florid face with its pointed chin is so full of character that one wonders, as the early collectors did, if he was not a portrait. His coloring is rich, with deep Van Dyke brown hair; his body is homemade and so is his clothing. The possession of a tall beaver hat implies that he once had a wardrobe.

By mid-century, the china-head dolls had become firm favorites. They were made by many different, anonymous factories, most of which, no doubt, were primarily concerned with more serious china products, and were distributed from Germany all over the world. The quality of the mid-century dolls, although more commercial or mass-produced than the early ones, is superb, and already showed a great variety of improvements and innovations. Dolls were made with glass eyes and real hair wigs; sometimes the heads were set on jointed wooden bodies, with or without china limbs. A few very desirable chinas were made as copies of complicated Japanese dolls, known as "Motschmanns" after the German patentee.

Some of the variations are to be seen in **illustration 2**. The little glass-eyed doll is of beautiful quality, one of a series made in a range of sizes. The brilliant blue glass gives the doll great vitality. The wooden-bodied doll is shown without her clothing, so that her smoothly-working wooden joints can be seen.

The "scrimshaw" doll shown here is unique, as far as we know. A New England sailor must have purchased the bisque doll's head while home on leave. Whaling ships were often away for a year and more, and during those long months, he whittled a wooden body for the doll, and carved the limbs from whale ivory. The head is nailed on in a rugged, no-nonsense manner, and the use of materials available at sea—the rubber tubing used for the joints and the thick iron wire—is very moving.

The china doll had become a nursery classic by the

I find the Marguerites enchanting, with their loose, impressionistic paint, offbeat colors and elusive, art nouveau quality, but apparently my enthusiasm is not shared.

1860's and we can see it becoming cheaper and more stylized. It is from this decade that the bulk of the molds originate. They were expensive, and the china factories continued to use them for years, making the dating of individual dolls difficult for collectors. Molds wear out with use, and after a while the heads lose the sharpness of their modeling. Thus it is possible to find two identical dolls with a 30-year difference in their ages, and an 1860 hairstyle may top an unlikely dress from the 1890's, which may be authentic and untouched. A good general rule is: the crisper the modeling, the closer the doll is likely to be to the date of the mold.

The 1860's saw, too, the growing popularity of the unglazed, or bisque, china dolls. These are often cast from the same molds as the glazed dolls, although the matte finish gives a very different effect. While most glazed chinas have enameled black hair, the bisques are usually blond, perhaps because the pale color accentuates the modeling. But the rare glazed blond dolls, like the one in **illustration 2**, are strikingly beautiful.

The late 1860's saw the development of the decorated or fancy bisque heads, with their elaborate coiffures and ornaments. Combs, flowers and leaves, ribbons and bows, tiaras, even birds and butterflies were molded or applied to ornament the hairstyles of these dolls, while their shoulders were often adorned with pleated blouses, ruffles, collars and necklaces. The delicate coloring is heightened with gilding and copper lustre, and although towards the 1880's the decoration may become too rich and gingerbread for some tastes, the finest of these fancy bisques have a lyrical quality and exquisite perfection that is comparable to any fine chinaware. They can be found with painted or inset glass eyes, with closed or open mouths, with fixed or swivel necks. The pair of heads on the right in **illustration 3** were cast from the same basic mold. Between them they bear most of these variations, and sport different hair ornaments.

The choice in this period is very wide, and again there is a paradox, for some of the commonest examples are among the most lovely. But there are plenty of unusual dolls including super-rarities like the baby girl in the bonnet and the boy in the military cap in the foreground of **illustration 3**.

By the 1880's the heyday of the china doll was over, and although they lingered on into the 1890's and even into the new century, they were no longer aristocrats, no longer new. But just at this time, when the chinas and especially the fancy bisques were on their way out, a variant appeared which was to be enormously popular for the next ten years or so.

Collectors call them "bonnet dolls," again not a very satisfactory name since they wear a bewildering variety of caps, hats, and even hoods. One old trade name for them was "hooded chinas." Essentially a cheap product, they are mostly of a coarse, granular bisque that has a curious charm of its own.

One group of these dolls, called "Marguerites" at the time, wears fantastic headgear resembling flowers and insects. Some of these can be seen in **illustration 4**: the apple blossom, the morning glory, the butterfly and the shamrock. I find the Marguerites enchanting, with their loose, impressionistic paint, offbeat colors and elusive, art nouveau quality, but apparently my enthusiasm is not shared. The Marguerites, indeed all the bonnet dolls, are neglected by collectors and are still very reasonably priced.

Until recently, china dolls had not found favor with collectors, though in the 1920's the "doll ladies" had a great fondness for the bisque counterparts, especially the elaborately ornamented ones. But even these fell from favor in the 1950's and 1960's, when the French Bébés took the collective imagination by storm, and research on American dolls shifted the emphasis still further.

Thoughtful articles by dedicated china lovers like Estelle Johnson, the Colemans and Frances Walker, have done much to bring the excellence of china dolls into general awareness. Mona Borger's splendid book, *Chinas: Dolls for Study and Admiration* (1983, Borger Publications), is the first serious attempt at classification in depth. It is a landmark, a sure sign of the slow change in taste.

Another sure sign is the sharp escalation in prices, especially for the earlier, rarer dolls. But it is still possible to find china dolls of top quality at surprisingly reasonable prices. Fashion, as I said, is a fickle business.

The collectors of the 1930's, eager for knowledge, tended to supply the facts for themselves. Not only was little known about these toys, but they were not considered very seriously, even by their collectors. Even the country of origin was not clear and today's collector, reading the old books, is often puzzled to find her classic German chinas referred to as "Staffordshire."

The term "pink lustre" was invented to describe glazed chinas with flesh tinting, together with a legend that gold was mixed with the pink color. The name "Parian" was coined to separate the finer, untinted fancy bisques from their coarser counterparts, even though these dolls are richly colored, and Parian implies a frosty whiteness. Most confusing of all, the collectors of those days invented a profusion of attributions, claiming that various dolls were portraits—Jenny Lind, Queen Victoria, Mary Todd Lincoln and so on. Most of these names have been dropped by today's better informed collectors. Names are necessary if we are to know what we are talking about—to say nothing of buying—but the perpetuation of inaccuracy is never advisable or desirable. Dolls and their collectors are still treated with amused tolerance by the rest of the world of decorative arts, and it is this amateurishness, particularly with regard to nomenclature, which is responsible.

Meanwhile, we can rejoice at the rediscovery of china dolls. They have many excellencies. They are typical of their period, and unlike woodens or waxes or even the later bisques, they do not change; their features and hairstyles and coloring are constant. They are often of great artistic merit, with superb modeling and character. Even the least of them is a work of fine craftsmanship. The best of them rank with the finest decorative acts of their day.

Until recently, china dolls had not found favor with collectors, though in the 1920's the "doll ladies" had a great fondness for the bisque counterparts, especially the elaborately ornamented ones.

The Mystery of Mary Cole

COULD THE AUTHOR'S UNSOPHISTICATED 18TH-CENTURY ENGLISH DOLL
BE ONE OF THE LEGENDARY "BARTHOLOMEW BABIES"?

As prinked-up and tawdry as a Bartholomew Baby!" Such was the derogatory catchphrase that described an overdressed, vulgar woman. It was in common use in the 18th century among all classes in England. Bartholomew Babies were cheaply made dolls that were sold in street fairs, and they take their name from the great winter fair that was held, every year, just before Christmas, outside Saint Bartholomew's Church in London.

The catchphrase was in use for a long time, and the dolls must have been made in very large numbers. But like the misnamed celluloid "Kewpie dolls" from 20th-century fairgrounds, they were frail, flimsy things, not meant to last for more than a day or two.

A great many dolls survive from the 18th century, of many different kinds, but so far we have no evidence to prove that any of them are the legendary Bartholomew Babies. I have sometimes suspected a common kind of wooden doll, a thoroughly commercial product, dressed in a stylized panniered dress, its skirts lined with paper, its wig a hank of twisted tow, its trimming always the same, tinseled, furnishing braid. These dolls have skirts of vertical patchwork, a curious convention. They are known in England as "bagmen's dolls," and there is some evidence that they were made as a sideline by joiners and turners, woodworkers who made furniture. This would certainly explain the dolls' patchwork skirts, which are thriftily contrived from the seam trimming of upholstery and curtain fabrics.

These dolls, of which Philadelphia's "Laetitia Penn" is an example and my own Museum of the City of New York's "Mary Jenkins" is another, still exist in large numbers, and they certainly exhibit the symptoms of cheap-

The author's 18th-century doll was found in her original homemade wooden case, as seen on the following page. When the case is opened, right, the doll's cheaply made shepherdess costume is revealed.

ness and quick mass-production, but they are dowdy rather than tawdry; they have a solid utilitarian quality, like the Grodner Tal woodens and the common chinas that followed them. They are homely dolls, singularly lacking in flamboyance.

I am an Englishman, with a nostalgic love for the English countryside, and for all the popular, "folk" arts of its past—the "unsophisticated arts" as Barbara Jones so aptly christened them. I have always been intrigued by the idea of Bartholomew Babies, and I have always hoped that I will someday find one tucked away in some forgotten corner.

A doll in a wooden case was offered at Richard Withington's auction house in Hillsboro, New Hampshire, some time ago. It inspired little interest, perhaps because the case had, unfortunately, been sadly damaged in transit, and the doll itself had had its nose smashed in, creating a clownlike disfigurement. My friend Richard Wright was able to secure it for me for quite a modest sum.

This doll interests me for several reasons. First of all, it is clearly untouched, except for the fadings of time. Secondly, it has its name and a very precise date, which for an early doll is like being born with a silver spoon in its mouth. On the back of the case, in large, archaic, painstaking letters, is written "Mary Cole" and "Sept 1759." The same inscription, in the same hand, can be made out very faintly under a later coat of dark varnish on the front panel of the case door.

Dolls set in shadowboxes, to be hung in the parlor in memory of dead children, were a common enough phenomenon in the early 19th century, when families were large and infant mortality frequent. Occasionally examples from the previous century are found, like the lovely one— a "bagmen's" doll—in the American Wing of the Metropolitan Museum of Art in New York.

Mary Cole's wooden case is a humble affair, obviously homemade. I was puzzled by the proportion of the glass; it is like a window in a sedan chair. It was Bishop Clement, the clergyman with whom I live, who pointed out that it was the exact size of a 12-pane window glass, and that the maker had used whatever was at hand. The case is lined roughly with a scrap of 18th-century wallpaper—something else to be hoarded and made use of.

The doll itself is made from coarse papier-mâché down to its waist, and is modeled to represent a fine lady. It has a fashionably narrow waist and pushed-up bosom. The features are the merest suggestion, and they are painted with bravura but without skill or refinement. The hips and legs are wood, with simple hip joints, and the waist is a thick

dowel, over which the papier-mâché waist is glued. The legs have been made very long, a trick to make the doll seem bigger, which recurs in the cheap German bisques of the early-20th century. An unexpected delight is Mary Cole's well-carved shoes, with the high heels and vamps and upcurving toes of the period. The arms, on the other hand, could not be cruder; they are just simple bunches of straw, wrapped in linen.

Such is Mary Cole's construction. She is dressed as a shepherdess, a fanciful conception derived from the highly decorated chinawares of Chelsea and Bow. Her petticoat is made of unbleached paper, coarse enough to be blotting paper, and it is nailed to the dowel, then crudely folded and stitched into panniers.

Next comes a second petticoat of cheap unbleached linen, and then the skirt of white cotton mull with a woven pane pattern and a printed lavender sprig. It has been made up with a very deep flounce. These two layers of the costume were sewn together to the paper pannier with long, rough stitches.

The bodice and its peplum are made from a scrap of sprigged wallpaper, overlaid with tissue paper that was originally a deep violet color. The stomacher is suggested by strips of gold tinsel. The sleeves have been contrived from the petticoat and skirt fabrics, and they are ornamented with ribbons of the violet tissue. There were once sprays of green tissue leaves at the shoulders. The shepherdess hat is blue paper, trimmed with cambric leaves and flowers, while the wig is contrived from a twisted strip of the petticoat linen. The decorated staff is a stick wrapped in wallpaper. The only material of any quality is the scrap of blond lace at the waist and at the décolletage, and the inch or so of black silk ribbon about the neck. This dress—indeed, the entire doll— has the slick, hasty look of cheap merchandise.

Originally this doll, with her violet and blue and gold, with her snowy mull and her unexpected, orange shoes, was colorful and showy, a doll to be sold in a noisy fairground, "as prinked-up and tawdry as a Bartholomew Baby." She was bought for Mary Cole, perhaps a farmer's child, who never played with her, who died in September 1759, and whose memorial, so lovingly contrived, hung in the parlor until our own times.

The damage has been carefully made good, with many bitter thoughts about the carelessness and the irresponsibility of those who condone, by lack of protest, the abuse and destruction of the fragile treasures that they profess to love. Mary Cole hangs in my parlor now, safe, at least for my time. I see her every day, and I remember the little girl who died so young, so long ago. And every day I wonder— have I, at last, found a real Bartholomew Baby?

The Doll that Lived Through the Siege of Paris

A COLORFUL PERSONAL HISTORY ADDS DRAMA AND VALUE TO A WELL-PRESERVED ANTIQUE

There are fashions in doll collecting, as in all long-lived human activities. These fashions are sometimes very noticeable, as when a new discovery is made or a new dollmaker appears. But there are also slowly moving changes in taste, which are perhaps predictable, but which can come about, so to speak, behind one's back.

In the early days of collecting—the 1920's and 1930's—much store was set upon provenance: where the dolls had come from, to whom they had belonged and what had been their history. The early doll books, those for instance of Janet Johl and Eleanor St. George, are full of such histories—the Doll that Went Through the Flood, the Doll that Belonged to the President's Daughter or the Crown Princess. Such stories have now fallen into disfavor, which seems to me a great pity. The reasons are not hard to find. Among enthusiastic amateur collectors, accessories and documents are easily lost as the dolls change hands, and what was once proof becomes hearsay. The truth, always fascinating and sometimes riveting, degenerates into distorted gossip, sentimental and unconvincing. Then, too, great strides have been taken in research during recent years, and the attention of the collector has become more focused on the doll as a good specimen, pure and anonymous, rather than as a personality in its own right.

About ten years ago, a doll was offered to the Museum of the City of New York. An early French lady doll, her glazed head bore the heavy features of a Huret, although her kid body was without identifying markings. She wore a splendid, homemade silk dress of the 1860's, complete with crinoline hoop, and an enchanting blue velvet bonnet. This doll came with a very large and elaborate trunk, with a child's name beautifully painted upon it. It bore several trays, and the lid was furnished with several compartments, all labeled in French—gloves, jewelry, etc. This trunk contained an elaborate wardrobe and many hats and shoes, jewel boxes and workboxes, toilet cases, umbrellas, parasols, traveling rugs—even a tea set of pretty, flowered porcelain, together with a carte-de-visite photograph of the child, Eugenia, with her mother. We were delighted, and were prepared to accept this treasure, but we are a history museum, and for us, provenance is of prime importance. All our accessions must have New York connections.

"Eugenia," as we for convenience called the doll, passed the New York connections test with flying colors. She was from a most interesting New York family. Moreover, as a bonus, she came with an exciting and moving personal history, carefully preserved, and handed down in the family, along with the doll.

For business reasons, the Tilton family had gone to live in Paris, France. They were well-to-do, and the child Eugenia was clearly disposed to luxury. Like her mother, she was a forceful and determined character. She must have had many toys, but on seeing this doll in an expensive Parisian toy shop, she declared that it was the only one that could make her happy. When her mother declared with equal firmness that such a purchase was out of the question, Eugenia persuaded her doting grandfather to join her in the morning walks, led

"Eugenia," opposite page, is an early French doll, possibly a Huret, named after her first owner, Eugenia Tilton. She is dressed in a homemade silk dress and velvet bonnet, in the style of the 1860's. She was given to the Museum of the City of New York with a large trunk containing an elaborate wardrobe and numerous accessories.

Gants

She was from a most interesting New York family. Moreover, as a bonus, she came with an exciting and moving personal history, carefully preserved, and handed down in the family, along with the doll.

him artlessly to the toy shop, and sighed sadly over the doll. Of course, her wiles were successful.

Mama, presumably, was resigned, for the story tells us that she joined forces with her lady's maid to make the doll's lavish wardrobe. The many rich accessories must have been subsequent presents, for some of them are a little later in date than the clothes.

Eugenia was to have a dramatic childhood, for the family was delayed in leaving Paris at the outbreak of the war with Prussia in 1870, and was trapped in the famous siege. The populace was reduced to near starvation. These must have been terrifying times for the sheltered little girl, with the ever-present threat of Prussian invasion. As evidence of the duress of the time, there is, among the doll's luxurious possessions, a hard, blackened little object, a crust of rye bread. Dramatizing—and perhaps softening—her hardships and anxieties by sharing them with her doll, Eugenia had also shared with it her meager rations, leaving behind for us a mute testament to her courage and her endurance. This story is recorded in the Tilton doll's accessions sheets at the Museum of the City of New York. I can only wish that more such intriguing family histories had been preserved.

As the collecting of old dolls becomes more popular and more expensive, the dolls' original purpose becomes more and more obscured. That they are now considered as decorative art of no insignificant order is not surprising—indeed, one is gratified that they are at last being treated with the respect which they surely deserve. But it is sad and alarming to see their original purpose ignored or dis-

missed. When the child is forgotten, the doll loses its integrity and much of its character. In this forgetfulness, inevitable restorations and renewals are downright destructive.

At the risk of being thought old-fashioned, I continue to look behind the wonderful dolls of the past, and to seek out the girls—and boys—for whom they were bought. And I am on the watch for family histories like Eugenia Tilton's, which bring the dolls, and the children who loved them, so vividly to life.

The Romantic Royal Wedding
Paper Dolls from the Past

THE AUTHOR DISCOVERED A SET OF HOMEMADE PAPER DOLLS WHICH
ARE SPLENDID EXAMPLES OF 19TH-CENTURY FOLK ART

Museums are, all of them, Aladdin's Caves; it is one of their most fascinating characteristics. However crisp and smart their galleries, however orderly and organized their storerooms, there are always backrooms, attics or basements, where objects not currently in focus, objects of dubious worth, or plain old misfits are tucked away, to fade slowly into oblivion. These caches of forgotten objects are often the bane of existence for young, inexperienced curators with stars in their eyes and dusters in their hands. And this is a pity, because such dusty boxes are today a prime source of new dis-

Lord Clarendon, left, is quite eclipsed by the splendor of the Mulgrave ladies. Our artist did not attempt to collage the Earl Marshall's robes, although she drew his orders and decorations in careful detail. Lady Mulgrave is well aware of our admiration.

coveries; yesterday's discards have a disconcerting way of turning into tomorrow's treasures.

It was in the attics of the Museum of the City of New York, in just such a dusty box, that I discovered the treasures depicted here. The box, which had been forgotten for years, contained dozens of handmade paper dolls, of all dates. They had been stored away in a perfunctory manner, in Museum envelopes, by a predecessor who presumably did not appreciate their charm. Tastes change with time, and often, what once looked like clumsy, amateur work now seems endearing, and can even be revealed as folk art of great merit. Many of these lost paper dolls were very beautiful to my eyes, but none of them prepared me for the surprise of the splendid set that represents the Wedding of the Princess Royal.

Queen Victoria was a monarch of unprecedented popularity. Not since the heyday of Queen Elizabeth the First had the Crown been so idolized. She had come to the throne at a time of great unrest, when her profligate uncles and the lingering war with France combined to bankrupt the country. The British were sick of kings, and revolution was in the air. But instead of a new king, a slim, straight girl of 18 with shy manners but a clear, direct gaze, ascended the throne, and soon won the hearts of her subjects. Three years later, she fell in love, surprisingly, with

Opposite page: The Marchioness of Clanricarde, left in photo, is impressive in white satin, ornamented with crimson and gold. She is accompanied by Lady Bessborough, who wears her brilliant crinoline of kingcup yellow with great complaisance. Its posies of gentians, forget-me-nots and polyanthus have been cut and assembled with exacting care. Not the least of the charm of these paper dolls is the way in which different expressions of the ladies have been captured.

The Duchess of Kent is regal in her purple velvet and ermine. Her train is carried by the Lady Anna Maria Dawson. The Duchess of Buccleuch wears mauve, the new court color, inspiring the envy of the ladies in the background

the consort who had been chosen for her.

Prince Albert of Saxe Coburg was indeed Prince Charming—young, handsome and dashing. But he was also big-hearted, gentle, intelligent and considerate. After a fairy-tale wedding, the couple settled down to live happily ever after, and they set the tone of domestic bliss for the rest of the country. Under their benign rule, Britain prospered, and ten years later, with the Great Exhibition, Prince Albert's brainchild, displayed its new affluence to the rest of the world.

The nation had taken their Royal Family to their hearts, and had begun that love affair with them which is today as true and constant as ever, inexplicable though it may seem to other countries. "They're our family!" my mother used to say to my American friends, who wondered at the photographs of the queen that hung beside her bed. And the British, of course, are enduringly—and, I hope, endearingly—sentimental, especially about animals and young love. When the queen's eldest daughter was betrothed in the 1860's, the country went as wild over the coming nuptiuals as it did recently over those of the Princes Charles and then Andrew. On the eventful day in the 19th century, the newspapers were almost entirely given over to the descriptions of the wedding, and a few days later the enormously long Court Circular was reprinted in its entirety in *The New York Times*.

And now, after this preliminary history lesson, we come to our paper dolls, for a little girl in New York, listening to her sisters reading aloud the details of the sumptuous wedding, pictured it vividly in her mind. "The ladies who occupied the seats prepared for the occasion," observed the Court Circular sedately, "the greater part of whom were in the bloom of youth, were all in full Court dress, and the dazzling effect of their jewels and feathers, their silks and laces, but above all, their natural charm, may easily be imagined." While her sisters sighed and dreamed of their own Prince Charmings, our little girl set to work with her pencil to bring the wedding into colorful existence.

"There were singularly few gentlemen among the spectators," remarked the Circular, with well-bred surprise. "The scene was therefore all color, tier upon tier, like a brilliant slope of flowers." Our little girl was determined to achieve this effect with her paper dolls, and she succeeded admirably.

She drew her dolls carefully on writing paper, with great economy of line, and great delicacy, her assurance and obvious pleasure in her task more than compensating for her lack of draftsmanship. Then, following the Court Circular's rapturous descriptions faithfully, she depicted the dresses in collage. She used both shiny flint and matte clay papers; she begged scraps of velvet, satin and lace from her sisters. She snipped gold and silver trimmings from cigar bands and discarded valentines. Tirelessly, she cut dozens of minute flowers from colored Christmas and trade cards, and enriched her dolls with tiny beads and wisps of tulle and feathers. She was obviously delighted with the results, and so perhaps were her sisters, for the dolls become increasingly elaborate, and the worker quickly developed an admirable dexterity. Her dolls certainly delight us today. I always took great pleasure in the ecstatic responses of visitors to my office to whom I showed the Royal Wedding dolls.

The newspaper pages, with their lavish description of the wedding, had been carefully saved with the dolls, and it is amusing to compare them. The dolls are easily identified, since the child wrote their names and titles on their backs. "Her Grace the Duchess of Buccleuch was wearing a magnificent robe of mauve, the new Court color," notes the Circular, and the paper doll wears the same new, rare color.

Our child clearly felt it her duty to include a few gentlemen as escorts, and she even depicted the archbishop, but they received scant attention. Lord Clarendon's plain blue suit, for instance, cannot hold a candle to the glory of the Ladies Mulgrave, with their wreaths and garlands of flowers.

The dolls depicted here, just a small part of the complete assemblage, show not only their glory, but also the wit and vitality of the artist. The posing of her ladies, the tilting of their heads and the quick darting of their eyes as they survey each other—all this is masterly portraiture, while the intricate folds of crinoline and train are contrived with economy and skill. The assembled wedding party is as fresh and lively as on the day when it was completed. In my opinion, it has the stature of a masterpiece of folk art.

I can only be thankful that my predecessor tucked this toy away, and that I was the lucky person to rediscover it. And I am endlessly thankful that museums, by their very nature, are all Aladdin's Caves. Now that I am retired, I am often invited to consult for other museums—to review their holdings in dolls and toys. And, whenever possible, I accept these invitations, hoping, of course, that I shall be given access to the backrooms, attics and basements, where, I feel certain, treasures such as the Royal Wedding Paper Dolls, lie sleeping.

The Yankee Doll

THE STORY OF THIS BISQUE WEARING A PATRIOTIC PRINT DEMONSTRATES THAT NOTHING IS EVER CERTAIN

When I first became curator of the famous Toy Collection of the Museum of the City of New York, I thought naively that the most important qualifications for my position were knowledge, a leaning towards scholarship and an orderly habit of mind. I was soon to learn that these virtues alone would not prevail, unless one were amply endowed with tact, foresight and a ripe understanding of human nature. Now, after 27 years of service, I find myself adding two other essential qualities to this daunting list—humility and an open mind.

The soundness of these conclusions can be judged by the case of the Yankee doll. I discovered this fascinating creature quite early in my survey of the museum's holdings and, as a newcomer to the U.S.A., I was greatly impressed by her. We are not taught American history in England, and my hazy knowledge of the Civil War had been culled from the movies. But here, surely, was a doll from Civil War days dressed in calico with a patriotic Yankee print. My understanding of the distinctions of Yankee character was also derived from the movies. I have always loved Katharine

Hepburn, and *Little Women* was vivid in my mind as I pondered on the implications of this doll.

Ours is a history museum and, strictly speaking, its collections should only include artifacts relating to New York history. All the toys in our collection have belonged at some time to New Yorkers, but those with a particular link with historic events are given more prominence. Thus I was delighted to find this doll, ordinary enough in itself, with its everyday blond bisque head and its cloth body, but remarkable and perhaps unique in that it preserves a patriotic impulse at a particular, historic moment. It was easy to imagine the young Mama, bereft and lonely for the husband newly departed for the war, first as she bought the exciting new calico for its printed soldiers, flags and cannons, and then as she proudly wore her new dress for the first time, her gesture of involvement. And of course the remnants of the calico would have been made up into an identi-

The Yankee Doll has a blond bisque head and a cloth body, and wears a calico dress printed with a patriotic motif.

cal dress for her daughter's doll—and how proudly the child would have shown it to her little friends.

The doll's dress has a very simple silhouette, and it is not a fashionable dress, but rather a morning or working costume—indeed, such washable print dresses were universally worn by house servants, as well as their mistresses, in the mid-19th century. The same silhouette is worn by the young ladies in Augustus Egg' painting of 1862, "The Travelling Companions," while the housemaid in Frank Stone's genre picture, "The Tryst," is wearing a dress identical to that worn by the doll.

During my time, the Civil War doll enjoyed great prominence at the Museum of the City of New York. She featured largely in my exhibitions, and she was often lent to other museums, as a romantic Civil War memento, together with the various dolls that were sold at the legendary Sanitary Fairs. Indeed, I have often wondered whether such a Fair was our Yankee doll's own origin, for she came to us with no documentation. We knew only that her name was "Maggie."

This is the simple story of "Maggie," the Yankee doll, in which I have always taken a proprietary pride, and this article would have ended with a valedictory paragraph, pointing out with smugness how yet again, a mere child's toy can illuminate vividly a cataclysmic moment in time. But since I began to prepare this article, some interesting facts have emerged, which make the story not so simple, and provide the new Curator of Toys, Jane Hirschkowitz, with a rich opportunity for research.

Jane is good friends with Kimberly Fink, a staff member of the Costume Institute of the Metropolitan Museum of Art in New York City. Kim has found in the Institute's collection a little boy's dress made from the same fabric as the Yankee doll's dress. The Institute dates the dress as circa 1850, and if this is true, it makes the interpretation of "Maggie" more complicated. Perhaps she may have worn this dress, blithely, for ten years or so before the Civil War began. On the other hand, Kim has discovered, in the Metropolitan's textile department, which is separate from the Costume Institute, a very similar fabric, used in a baby's dress of circa 1862. The department has

The boy's ecru cotton dress bears the same print as the doll's dress, and it is dated 1850 by The Costume Institute. (Boy's dress; The Metropolitan Museum of Art/gift of Mrs. Samuel Schwartz)

determined that this textile was printed at the American Printworks in Fall River, Massachusetts. If the dating here is correct, then this dress, at least, was made after the Civil War began.

The dating for both costumes is conjectural, however, and Kim plans to research both the garments and the textiles. In doing so she will have to take into account, as Jane and I have, the maddening elasticity of time and place. There is a time lag in fashions, for instance, so that a working woman in New England might easily wear in the mid 1860's the dress that Frank Stone's housemaid wore in England some five or six years earlier. And while hundreds of patterns of great richness were produced by Victorian fabric mills, these patterns were apt to stay current for a disconcerting length of time. For that matter, the very head of our Yankee doll, simple and classic, was produced over too many decades for the comfort of doll historians. (And, in addition, very recently, in fact, Jane discovered at the museum one more small piece of this doll's history—a battered nightdress with a handwritten note pinned to it, indicating that it belonged to "Maggie.")

Personally, I am delighted with these new discoveries. While they do not exactly disprove the Yankee doll's claim for a Civil War provenance, they leave her open to questions, which is always healthy. And besides, now that my reactions can be legitimately independent, I can indulge my own pleasure in the Yankee character—in its independence, its regional pride, its peculiarly English heritage, and of course its thriftiness. Yankees, we understand, never throw anything away—the ladies of Boston have their hats, just as they have their antiques and their untouched family houses. Indeed, it may be this New England thriftiness that has preserved our doll for us, in such pristine condition.

If I were writing a label for this doll today, I would have to say, "Almost certainly dressed during the Civil War, in a patriotic fabric." But without hesitation I would label her a Yankee doll. She is, through my English eyes, at least, a Yankee through and through.

...E AUTHOR ADMITS TO BEING BLIND TO ...RES SET UNDER HIS VERY NOSE

...king, I ...prid- ...But ...ler-...se for mor...

They... her parlo... dome on a... that I live... Dixon and... very often. M... that the parl...

head still reels as I sit there. It is hard to drink tea calmly, and make small talk, in a room that holds an armoire full of 18th-century woodens, a tin dollhouse stuffed with tin furniture, a musical, mechanical sewing box, and an 18th-century mechanical dollhouse—indeed a whole cupboard crammed with rare and marvelous mechanicals. Further to excuse my blindness, the little dolls appeared at Christmas, when they had to compete with all sorts of new delights, including no less than four of Winnie

These tiny antique parians, posed in a game of Blind Man's Bluff, have bodies and legs molded in one piece, but their ...ms are jointed and swiveling. Each has its own bisque stand.

Langley's incredible Christmas trees.

All the same, it was not until April that the little dolls were brought gently to my attention. "I've been talking to Jane Hirschkowitz, at the museum in New York," I said as I put my cup down. (To those readers who might not be familiar with her name, Jane is the curator of the toy collection at the Museum of the City of New York.) "We've been looking for subjects for articles for *Dolls* magazine."

"Oh, what were you looking for?" asked Dorothy.

"Something small and rare and delicious—some-

All the dolls in this Blind Man's Bluff set are about three inches high and wear their original factory-made costumes. A few have molded hats, and among these are a pair dressed in Tyrolean peasant costumes and a boy in a Scottish kilt. It seems clear that an entire group of such dolls representing a fancy-dress party must have been produced. The little boy who is the Blind Man has a molded blue blindfold around his head.

thing that could be easily overlooked," I said, and Dorothy laughed. "Why don't you use some of my stuff?" she twinkled. "Why don't you write about those all-bisques at your elbow?" And she took off the glass cover, and set out the little dolls under my nose. And at last I saw them.

In fairness to myself, I must admit that, crowded together they look, at first glance, like everyday all-bisques—nice early ones, with molded blond hair and sometimes hats, like the beautiful little jointed German bisques that were at their best in the late 1860's and early 1870's. I have always adored them, and long ago collected six or seven beauties to live in an 1860 dolls' room.

But now I saw how different Dorothy's little dolls were. They represent children at a party, playing Blind Man's Bluff. The little boy who is the Blind Man has a molded blue blindfold tied around his head, and his hands have been modeled in an open, out-reaching gesture. His companions are dodging him, and their legs are molded in dancing and running positions. Hands are clenched with excitement, or reach out—one girl with a delicately extended little finger—to touch him. The dolls all have jointed, swiveling arms, but their bodies and legs are molded in one piece. Each doll is provided with a little bisque stand, with a pin that fits neatly into a hole in the lower torso, to hold the doll upright. All the dolls wear their original, factory-made costumes. They are dressed in party clothes. A few have molded hats, and among these are a pair dressed in Tyrolean peasant costumes, and a boy in a Scottish kilt.

"I have seen two more," said Dorothy. "And I've been hoping for years that their owner will get tired of them. They are a boy and a girl dressed as Laplanders."

"Oh, but that means that there must have been still more," I said. "There must have been a whole fancy-dress party—Scottish, Irish, Spanish . . ."

"Oh, I expect so," said Dorothy, and she chuckled again. "I'm always looking out for them. I expect I'll run into others sooner or later."

"So you didn't get them all together, as a set?" I asked, and Dorothy laughed at me. "You do want things easy, don't you?" she said, as she gathered up the teapot. A new thought struck me. "How long did it take you to collect this many?"

"About 30 years!" she replied, as she disappeared into the kitchen.

Now this, to my mind, is the very peak and pleasure of collecting—to find a treasure so unusual and rare that most people have never noticed it, and then to pursue it, quietly and steadfastly, for half a lifetime. Sooner or later, Dorothy will find—or hear of—the rest of her set of Victorian party children and some day she will find a catalog or advertisement that will explain what they were called and who made them. Meanwhile, you can be sure that from now on I sit in Dorothy and Winnie's parlor drinking tea with my eyes peeled!

The Auctioneers' Mistakes

OR

HOW TO COLLECT DOLLS IF YOU ARE VERY, VERY POOR

Once, long ago in England, I read with great amusement in the very glossy English version of *House and Garden* magazine an article entitled "How to Deal with Christmas if You are Very, Very Poor." The author explained with some condescension that the reader should not bother to read on if he or she was comfortably situated. This advice was intended for the very, very poor, who found it an ordeal every Christmas to make ends meet. "Let us start with the servants," wrote the author graciously. "It is always best to give them money. . . ."

Clearly, poverty is relative, depending on one's standpoint. For most of my life I have been very, very poor, at least by my standards, if not by those of *House and Garden* magazine. And poverty has always been a great inconvenience since, from the age of six, I have been passionately seeking out and collecting old toys—games and puzzles, toy theaters, picture books and pop-ups and paper dolls, dollhouses and, of course, the dolls themselves. Poverty was no help.

In the beginning, when I was a schoolboy and later, as an art student, I haunted street markets and junk shops with my saved-up pocket money, and bought old toys instead of new toys, or candy or comics. By the time I had become a schoolteacher and at long last had an income, I owned both a collection of old toys and a collection of old

In spite of the soaring prices of recent years, those armed with sharp eyes and steady vigilance can still discover unusual and low-priced treasures, such as these two miscataloged dolls.

dolls, modest, but much loved.

This humble beginning taught me several important rules, by which I have collected every since. First of all, since I often found nice things that I could not afford, I learned very early to be tempted only by the best—by the things that kept me awake at night with longing, without which life did not seem worth living. And for those things I saved and schemed. I never borrowed, but I learned to trade up, to part with several or even many, lesser toys in order to acquire one splendid one.

Described in the catalog as a milliner's model, this doll turned out to be a Grodner Tal with a molded plaster head.

Thus from the start my collections have always been small—indeed, by some people's standards too small to be called collections. But even within so narrow a compass, I still regularly apply my second rule, which is to weed ruthlessly. As I explained in this magazine some months ago, my treasures are a daily delight, but if the delight begins to fade, then the fading piece goes on its way—long before delight turns to apathy—to provide the means of acquiring something new and vibrant, usually something earlier and better.

...my treasures are a daily delight, but if the delight begins to fade, then the fading piece goes on its way...to provide the means of acquiring something new and vibrant, usually something earlier and better.

The third rule in this magical how-to doctrine is to look, with sharp eyes and steady vigilance, in all sorts of unexpected places where dolls can sometimes be found. The fourth rule is to search carefully, in crowded antique shops or auction rooms, places where similar objects are herded together, for the occasional over-looked and mislabeled rarity. These rules apply, of course, to every field of collecting, and when I was younger and had a small antiques business, my rules brought me many rewards. In the field of toys these rules brought better results 20 years ago, before doll and toy collecting took off and prices soared. But there are still fantastic bargains to be found, for those with sharp eyes, by following my third and fourth rules.

Shown here are two rare dolls, both of them bought within the past few years. They were found at those huge auctions in New England that attract most of the collecting world from both sides of the Atlantic, and both were sold for a song, because they were inaccurately described in the catalogs. I withhold the names of the auction houses to spare the blushes of the owners and their catalogers, but I rush to say in their defense that there were hundreds and hundreds of dolls being offered (even whole boxes-full in one lot) and with such a formidable task to perform within a deadline, it is understandable that there will be a few inaccuracies. Those are just what I look out for. (There are other knowledgeable collectors with far sharper eyes than mine, but in the instances of these two dolls, I was very lucky, for no one else seemed to have noticed them.)

My first little doll was offered in the catalog as a "milliner's model." It was dirty and crumpled, one arm

was loose in its sleeve, and great chunks of paint and gesso were missing from the back of its head. "What on earth do you want that for?" said antiques dealer Richard Wright, who was bidding for me. "You've already got much better ones."

But once the doll was mine, and I had undressed it, it was quite clear why I had wanted it. For it is not a milliner's model with a papier-mâché head and a leather body with stiff wooden limbs. This is a Grodner Tal, a jointed wooden doll with articulated elbows and knees. The carving of the body is most unusual, and its hips have swiveled ball joints, so that the doll's feet can be turned out, like a ballet dancer's.

But the cataloger's error was justified, perhaps, because instead of the usual, smoothly carved head with painted hair and eyes, this doll has an alien, molded plaster head with a very elaborate, asymmetrical hairstyle. Many of the papier-mâché-headed milliners have this type of hairstyle, which dates from the mid-1820's. The loose arms and the flaking on the back of the head are still awaiting repair, but the doll's underwear, dress and apron have been professionally wet-cleaned and pressed. They are all original, very finely made, and date from the early 1830's. They add greatly to the value of this treasure.

The second doll was found at a similar, mammoth auction. She was at the back of a shelf of china dolls, which were lined up three deep. Her bisque head is a very pretty but common example from the 1870's, its blond hair ornamented with a molded black ribbon. (This same head is sometimes found with elaborate, applied flowers and other decorations, and it is then, of course, a very different matter.) This doll was wearing a crude homemade dress with a completely circular skirt, which gave it something of a fairground appearance, and this perhaps would account for its catalog description. I had passed by before I read that descrip-

tion, but I soon turned back to seek out the doll, for the catalog described it as having a "crude wooden body with celluloid limbs," and it struck me as wildly unlikely that any doll of this period, however common, would ever have been given celluloid limbs.

I examined the doll carefully, then thrust her back again into the ranks, and hoped that no one else would notice her. Apparently they didn't, and she became mine, again for a song. "What on earth did you want that for?" said Richard once more, and with great pleasure, I showed him. Under the ugly dress, the "celluloid" limbs were scrimshaw, handcarved whale ivory. This is the sort of mystery doll in which I take the utmost delight, and it was not difficult, from the evidence in front of me, to reconstruct her story.

The doll's head must have been bought by a Yankee seaman on shore leave, and taken off to sea with him to be turned into a doll for a little sister, perhaps, or a daughter. Whaling ships in those days were away for months, sometimes years, and the sailors practiced all kinds of crafts to while away their few leisure hours. Scrimshaw was especially popular, since the whalebone and ivory were readily available, and sailors made all sorts of useful and ornamental things, usually as gifts for loved ones. I have seen enchanting dolls' furniture, for instance, beds and chairs and chests, all made with great skill from this unlikely material.

Our sailor scoured his ship to find the other raw materials that he needed. He whittled the body from a turned wooden rod—perhaps a broken spar—and carved very accurately the recess where the molded shoulders were to fit. He fastened the head in place by running screws through the sewing holes, holding his breath, I am sure, lest too much pressure should crack the china. He carved the limbs very carefully, jointing the knees and defining with exquisite detail the delicate fingers. He painted the shoes a cheerful red. His paint was thick, outdoor stuff, but he put it on very thinly and carefully. His patience with all his clumsy materials is very touching. The legs are strung into their carved sockets with thick wire; the upper arms are made from coarse rubber tubing, dry and hard now, and held to the body by nails threaded with white glass beads.

This very unusual doll now wears nice, homely old clothes of the right date and style. They are clean and neat, and I think they suit her perfectly. For me, she is a very special treasure but I often think when playing with her (and she is delightful to play with) how very much more precious she must have been to the little Yankee girl who was her first owner. How surprised and delighted she must have been when the doll was first produced, with much pride, from our sailor's kitbag.

Like most people who have grown up very, very poor, I have always dreamed of becoming very, very rich—and I have not yet, by any means, given up the hope. I would be so very good at being rich, you see. I know exactly what I would do with Noble's Millions, and among the other delicious projects I look forward to amassing the most wonderful collection of dolls ever seen—the earliest, the rarest, the most vibrantly beautiful dolls that at present I dare not even look at, except in museums, or millionaires' collections. But I doubt if they would give me the pleasure that my modest little collection gives me today, especially the dolls, like the two described here, which were the rewards for sharp eyes and indefatigable searching, dolls that cost so very little and mean so very much.

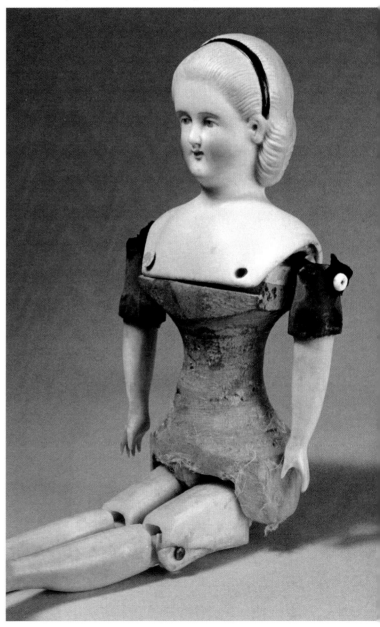

French, Handsome and Well-Heeled

THE AUTHOR VISITS A MYSTERIOUS GENTLEMAN WHO DOESN'T BELIEVE IN TRAVELING LIGHT

A mong today's dolls it must surely be the immortal Barbie who wins the prize for the sheer quantity of possessions that she has collected during her lifetime. She has clothes and accessories—which include her patient and presumably besotted boyfriend—for every conceivable occasion or profession. She has jewels and furs and automobiles, and her closets are bursting with impediments for every known sport. She must be the only doll ever to be provided by her indulgent creators with real estate—which includes, among other desirable properties, her dream house, her cocktail lounge, her private Lido and her very own theater.

Of course, there are antique dolls who can give Barbie a run for her money. I could list several 18th-century wooden heiresses who sit complacently in their Palladian dolls' mansions, surrounded by splendid furniture and well-trained doll-servants. Many of their lesser sisters, too, have come down over the years with their initialed trunks or their papered bandboxes. These often contain, besides alternative dresses, a cloak, a fan, a watch or a silver spoon, or an embroidered hussif complete with thimble, needles and thread; one

marvels that these pretty things should have stayed together for so long.

In the early 19th century, smoothly-jointed Grödner Tals were often endowed with wardrobes. Their high-waisted dresses are exquisitely sewn and embroidered, and are often accompanied by bonnets and bouquets and other enchanting accessories. Indeed, these dolls were often dressed as peddlers, who could collect in their baskets delicious, handmade trifles by the dozen.

Such collectors' delights seem usually to be English, although many similar dolls, as well as their papier-mâché or rag sisters, were at the same time amassing possessions in America, especially in thrifty New England. One demure little glass-eyed papier-mâché traveled, during the 1850's, in a pioneer wagon from New York to the newly opened Midwest. It was a long tedious journey, and the little doll collected a large wardrobe, stitched for her by well-wishers in neighboring wagons, on whose hands and hearts the long, tedious hours lay heavy. There was a tinker traveling with them, and he presented the doll with a beautiful hooded cradle, which he had fashioned from tin, and which was furnished, before the end of the journey, with no less than three pieced patchwork quilts.

Most of the possessions of these early dolls were handmade, even homemade. But by the middle of the 19th century, a new kind of doll had been invented in France, a lady doll with a head and sometimes limbs of fine porcelain, in both glazed and bisque versions. They were by no means cheap toys, but they were eminently desirable, and enormously successful. Status symbols, they were dressed in the height of Parisian fashion and

for them, for the first time, accessories were commercially made and could be bought along with the doll and her clothes.

These French luxury dolls can certainly give Barbie a run for her money. They were in their heyday during the 1860's and 1870's, an extravagant period, and there seems to be no end to the delightful accessories with which they were provided. Such dolls, when they survive with their documentation, provide invaluable insights into the modes and manners of their time and place. A charming and amusing example is the wedding couple which I once owned, and which is pictured in my book, *A Treasury of Beautiful Dolls* (Hawthorn Books, 1971). These dolls were a 12th birthday present in 1876, to Mabel Gray Potter, who lived in Oakland, a small town in Maine. Understandably, the wedding dress is made not from satin or silk, but from warm cashmere, and the going-away dress, together with sundry crocheted jackets and shawls, are all of wool. This little bride, named "Ethel," has many presents, and a handsome collection of jewelry. "Frederick," her bridegroom, on the other hand, came down to me with only one possession—a riding crop. Someone, I fancy, had a sense of humor.

Most of these luxurious French dolls were ladies, but a number of gentlemen do exist, some of them, like "Frederick," sporting top hats, canes or umbrellas, while

the soldiers among them—who, of course, are always officers—will wear their swords and sometimes medals. But it was not until recently, in California, that I made the acquaintance of the gentleman depicted here, whose possessions are positively mind-boggling.

To begin with, the doll himself is most unusual. His body is an elegant, articulated wooden one with bisque hands, and although this construction is endemic to these French dolls, it is rare and very desirable. His striking head is extremely beautiful and perhaps unique. It is unmarked, but its owner wonders if it might have been made by Huret, exhibiting as it does both the sensitive modeling and the haunting evocation of personality that are attributes of that manufacture. This handsome gentleman needs two trunks, a chest and a carpet bag to contain his belongings. One enviable trunk is covered with deerhide and lined with newspaper. A most suitable engraving of a standing lion, illustrating an advertisement, has been centered on the lid, proving, I feel, that someone else was aware of our gentleman's superb personality.

Lists can be daunting, but I propose to describe the

Opposite page: We know from his medals that our gentleman has seen military service; his chessboard suggests innocent amusement, his telescope, lofty intellect. Below: The newspaper lining of one of this gentleman's deerhide-covered trunks features an engraving of a standing lion, centered on the lid.

contents of this luggage in detail, since they are not only, collectively, a remarkable phenomenon, but because they shed much light on the character of our mysterious stranger. To begin—or perhaps to end with—our handsome friend possesses a cambric nightshirt (en suite with a nightcap) and a luxurious silk Japanese kimono—a classic man's indigo-colored one—to wear over it. His woolen vest is perhaps mundane, but his long drawers are made of scandalous silk. His *déshabillé* is completed by a beautiful, doll-sized paisley shawl.

To aid him in his toilet, this gentleman has an ivory hairbrush and a tortoiseshell comb, a straight razor, a toothbrush and clothes brushes, a shoehorn and a button hook. He has both woolen and silk stockings, four finely tailored shirts and a snowy starched one for formal occasions. His outerwear comprises a smart gray cutaway, and for inclement weather he has two umbrellas. Significantly, his evening clothes are the ones in which he seems to be most at ease, and he wears a splendid suit of tails, complete with top hat, cane and white kid gloves. He must once have owned other suits of clothes, for his accessories hint at a rich, full life, crowded with engagements and employments of many kinds. For instance, he is clearly an enthusiastic sportsman. He owns a riding crop and cap, a tweed shooting hat and chamois gloves which, together with his guns and binoculars, speak for themselves. He owns, too, a fishing reel, a net, a bait-and-tackle bag and a fishing umbrella, besides serviceable gumboots. He skates, too, and surely cuts a dashing figure on the ice—which may account for his silver trophy cup.

He has only one book, and a pair of spectacles—although I doubt that he needs them. He carries a chessboard, suggesting innocent amusement, but also a case with playing cards, and dice, which give us pause. His set of traveling champagne trumpets, together with his rapier and his very businesslike case of dueling pistols, confirm our apprehensions while bestowing on him an even more dazzling glamour.

> We know that he has seen military service, for his sword, his shako and his epaulets survive, and a box of medals implies bravery or perhaps, knowing our gentleman, foolhardiness.

He is unmistakably French, this gentleman—oh, how I wish I knew his name, for it is surely not Pierre or Jean! I can imagine something very romantic and unexpected, Hyacinthe, perhaps. And I am sure he has a title. His enigmatic face is both sensual and sad, a combination that is always irresistible. I suspect he broke the hearts of Parisian lady dolls wherever he went.

This suspicion deepens into certainty when one discovered his dancing slippers and his dance card, together with his knitted silk dancing gloves. He attended the opera, of course, with his cloak and his opera glasses, and there he surely took many a young lady doll's mind away from Offenbach.

His well-equipped writing desk—paper and envelopes, pen, penknife and paperknife (ivory), seal and sealing wax, ink pots and ruler—suggests a constant exchange of *billets doux*, while the box of postage stamps provides for future ones. It would be indiscreet to peep into his photograph albums, with their brass bindings and clasps.

On the other hand, our gentleman has tickets to the Myrioptican, which reveals a fondness for younger siblings, while his telescope hints at a lofty intellect beneath his dashing exterior. We know that he has seen military service, for his sword, his shako and his epaulets survive, and a box of medals implies bravery or perhaps, knowing our gentleman, foolhardiness. His bandana, I must admit, betrays a certain Bohemian streak, but his galoshes and his traveling rug suggest caution, and his pipes (three of them) and his paisley shawl imply an unexpected love of home comforts. To round out this multifaceted personality, his gold watch, watch chain and fob combine with his effulgent ensemble of luggage to suggest background and substance—qualities as much revered by Frenchmen in his day as in our own.

I have never met up with another Parisian gentleman doll who owned such a wardrobe, although they surely must exist—or must have existed. It is fortuitous that this, possibly the only one extant, should be so richly endowed, both with fascinating possessions and with a haunting, personal charisma that is just as fascinating.

The handsome French stranger's two trunks of clothing and accessories hint at a rich, full life, crowded with engagements and employments of many kinds.

PART II
1989-1992

By the late 1980s, the author had retired
to Southern California, where he delighted
in exploring the dolls in his neighbors'
collections, as well as his own.

A Moppet, A Poppet,
A Dainty Darlyng

AN INQUIRING LOOK AT A RARE OLD DOLL, WHICH TRANSPIRES TO BE
SOMETHING OF AN 18TH-CENTURY SURPRISE PACKAGE

Rarity, mystery, the ability to surprise, to open doors for the inquiring mind—these are some of the qualities that make a doll irresistible for me. And these are all qualities possessed by the innocent wooden doll depicted here. It represents a baby, dressed in formal long clothes—"a moppet, a poppet, a dainty darlyng"—as an old song says. It is not the only 18th-century baby doll known, but these are so extremely rare that to come upon one is in itself surprising and exciting.

To discover why there are so few babies among the 18th-century dolls that survive today, we need to inquire into social manners and attitudes. The latter half of the 18th century felt the rumblings of great change, literally the changeover from the old, insular, handmade world of the past to the interacting, machine-governed world in which we still live. It is not surprising that when we look at the first half of that century, we look at a culture quite remote from our own.

The doll here is difficult to date without documentation but it can, I think, safely be placed at about 1740 to 1750, the mid-century. At this time the child's world was a very different place from the carefully arranged environment that we have created for our own children. Our magical, golden nursery world literally did not exist. Small children were treated as babies until they ceased to toddle, but after that, at

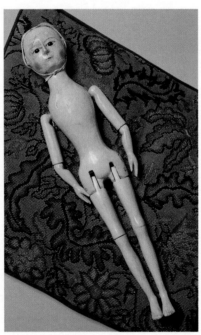

The natural waistline and mere suggestion of a bosom on this 18th-century wooden doll establish that it is meant to represent a child rather than an adult.

what would seem to us an alarmingly tender age, they became grown up, wore miniature versions of grown-up clothing and were given grown-up responsibilities.

This world of the 18th century was still sharply divided by class distinctions. There were the aristocrats and the gentry, who could be recognized because it was they who owned the land, and there was everybody else: the craftspeople and tradespeople, the farmers and laborers. None of the children, from either side of the division, knew the safe, protected state that we call childhood. The children of tradespeople and workers had to learn their skills or their trades and, in their small ways, contribute. The children of the gentry had yet more to learn. The son of a gentleman had to know how to manage his estate, take care of his land and look to the welfare of his tenants, while his sister had to know how to run her household and control her servants. Since she might well be married by the time she was 12, she had no time to waste.

Thus we can see that children of the 18th century led busy lives. But we must not assume that those lives were joyless, although toys were few and primitive by our standards. If the children of that time were more adult than those of the same age today, their parents were paradoxically more childlike than most adults are

the daughters of gentlemen, or for those who aspired to be mistaken for such. Their place in the life of their owner was that of companion and confidante, perhaps even of role model—the place that Barbie and her like occupy in the lives of little girls today. The cuddly toy and the baby doll to be nursed and cosseted are conspicuous by their absence. Another significant reason may well have been the abundance of babies in everyone's lives in those days. Perhaps there was no need for baby dolls in homes already teeming with babies!

During my perambulations about the world over half a century, in the course of my random and spasmodic poking and prying into museums' storerooms and other people's cupboards (which, when done by a more organized person, might be considered research), I have found very few real baby dolls, or even dolls dressed as babies, dating from the 18th century. And many of those discovered turn out, upon investigation, to be church figures or even, like the beautiful early wax infant pictured on page 28 of Mary Hillier's *The History of Wax Dolls* (1985, Hobby House Press), a funeral effigy. The few real examples that I have found could be viewed only through a glass case, or sometimes reverently held for only a few moments. So I am especially delighted by the Dainty Darlyng depicted here. He is in a collection in California, not far from my home, and his owner not only brought him to my house to be photographed, but volunteered to undress him.

So little is known about the dolls of this period that we do not have even newly invented names for the different varieties which we are beginning to discover. Our Moppet is one of a group of finely made

today. Even the educated and cultured were amused by what we should now consider infantile diversions—crude practical jokes, simple toys like jumping jacks and paper dolls. This is something I try to remember when confronting what I assume to be a child's toy from this period, for it might well have belonged to a married man or woman—even to someone of my own age!

Since childhood as we know it did not exist, it is not surprising that few dolls made as babies should exist, when few dolls represent children at all, except perhaps in dollhouses. Most of the dolls that survive from this era represent ladies. They were intended for

The gown, instead of being pinned together in the front, as was the standard mode for dressing babies (and ladies) in the 18th century, is fastened very sensibly in the back with tying tapes. Beneath the gown, the baby wears many layers of clothing. Next to his skin is a shift, a woolen petticoat, a corded linen petticoat and a waist-length "blouse," with a low neckline, which coincides with the neckline of the gown.

dolls that appear to have originated in England. Their faces are subtly carved, and their beautifully jointed bodies have distinctively forked hips and somewhat swollen-looking knees. Most have waists carved into fashionably corseted silhouettes, but a rare few have natural waistlines and only a suggestion of a bosom. This implies that these latter dolls were intended to represent children and, sure enough, our Moppet, when undressed, revealed this elegant, youthful body. There is no attempt at all to represent a real baby, but this is not surprising, since the only 18th-century wooden babies that I have seen were unmistakably church figures, and represented the Christ child. But whoever bought this Moppet originally took the trouble to choose one with the most piquant, whimsical expression, which it still wears 250 years later.

The only other examples that I can remember (but my memory these days is atrocious) which have been examined closely are recorded in the Colemans' *The Collector's Book of Dolls' Clothes* (1975, Crown Publishers). One is in the Victoria and Albert Museum in London, and the other in the Gallery of English Fashion in Manchester, both in England. Both are wooden, both from the same period as our Moppet. Both wear shifts and diapers and flannel petticoats. The London doll has two flannels and another of linen, and the Colemans distinguish these three garments as "undercoats," implying attached bodices. The silk gowns worn by these two dolls are cut like ladies' open robes, and are fastened at the bodice, the skirts remaining open. The London doll also wears mittens and a lace-trimmed bib; the Manchester doll has a long scarf of lace. To quote the Colemans:

Characteristically, the clothes on both dolls are pinned together, following the mode of dressing babies in the 18th century . . . The 1709 Tatler described one person's supposed memories of being dressed by the nurse who "took upon her to strip and dress me anew, because I made a noise . . . she did so and stuck a pin in every joint about me . . . I still cried . . . and, to quiet me, [she] fell a-nailing in all the pins by clapping me on the back."

With all this in mind, we turn back to our undressed Moppet. We were given the rare opportunity to examine his clothes, and here comes the surprise promised in the title, for the manner of his dress is quite different from that of either of the two other dolls. Next to his skin, he wears a shift, as long as his gown, cut with the classic folded-down flap in front. Over this he wears a woolen petticoat with a flannel weave, which is probably homespun. This garment ties at the back, but the seam is left open, and all the edges are lavishly bound with silk, an inch wide. Over this again comes a second long petticoat, this one made of most beautiful corded linen.

But it is his next two garments that constitute the surprise, for over his shift he wears something which one might think of as a shirt or a blouse, if one found it by itself. It is waist length, with a low neck which matches that of his shift, and long, full sleeves caught in at the cuffs. Both the neck and the cuffs are trimmed with narrow lace. Over this, he wears a long gown of fine lawn with a woven stripe. The Colemans say the gowns of dolls in England are "not as long as some of the baby dresses of the 19th century," but this is not true of our Moppet's gown. He too wears a long lace-trimmed bib reaching to his waist, but it is quite impractical, since it is completely covered with vertical lace ruffles and is obviously just for show. Like the silk gowns worn by the exam-

The baby wears a long gown of fine lawn, most likely his christening gown, and a beautifully quilted cap.

ples in England, this is probably his christening dress, which in the 18th century served an important, subsidiary purpose.

The safe birthing of a child was an event to be thankful for, in those days of primitive medicine, and it was attended with pomp and ceremony such as we nowadays accord to weddings. In the houses of the gentry, a bedroom was purposely set aside, and decorated with fine furnishings only matched by those of the drawing room. This was called the "lying-in room," and here the mother recovered from her ordeal, dressed in her finest nightgown and cap, and received visits, presents and congratulations from all her friends and relatives. It was an occasion for display, and the new infant lay in a fine cradle in his christening gown, the center of the festivities.

I digress from my surprise, which comes when we examine this fine gown, for it is cut exactly like a gown for a fashionable lady of the time, Here is the long, uncompromising bodice with its straight neckline dictated by the shape of the lady's corset, here are the back panels cut extremely narrow, and only wearable with the upright stance imposed by that corset. The sleeves come to the elbow, and are edges with three rows of lace frills, just like a lady's sleeves. (It is interesting to note here that the lace on the bib and that on the sleeves are identical, proving that the two garments were made en suite). The only difference between this gown and one for a lady of the period is that ladies' dresses closed in front, while this baby's gown closes at the back. And here is the second surprise, for—excepting a solitary one at the back of the neck of the shift—there is not a pin to be seen! Instead, this Moppet's gown, together with all his other garments, is fastened, very sensibly, with tying tapes. As yet, I have no way of knowing whether this method of fastening is unique to this doll, or a regional variant. It is certainly more comfortable and, surely, safer than those armories of straight pins! Our Moppet's costume is completed by the most beautifully quilted cap, so exquisitely sewn that one would suspect it of being intended for a real baby, were it not much too small.

The doll has returned to his owner, but I can sit and gaze at the photographs, and ponder and marvel to my heart's content. Here was rarity, here indeed were surprises and doors opened for the inquiring mind. And, for me the best of all, here was a tantalizing glimpse into a world long vanished, whose ways are barely and imperfectly remembered. Folk songs provide other glimpses, and—if I knew the tune—I could sing now that lullaby, which ends with the refrain: "A moppet, a poppet, a dainty darlyng!"

The Hat-Tippers' Ball

A GATHERING OF VERY RARE DOLLS WHOSE PURPOSE IS A MYSTERY— AT LEAST TO THIS AUTHOR

D o you like my new hat?" my sister would ask. "It was very expensive; it came from Paris!" Or, "Isn't my new perfume lovely? It's French—it cost the earth!" Ever since I can remember, "French" meant luxury, and "Parisian" implied sybaritic living.

During the early 19th century, a bankrupt France had very cleverly developed and exploited its many luxury products. The last quarter of that century was, for most of Europe, a time of prosperity and by 1875 women all over the world were saying, just as my sister did in the 1930's:

"Do you like my new hat? It came from Paris!" Never before had such lavish and luxurious merchandise been offered—or to a more appreciative, pleasure-loving public.

The famous Parisian toy shops—Le Nain Bleu, for instance, or Le Singe Violet—were at this time stuffed to overflowing with costly and enchanting dolls of every description. I for one never cease to marvel at their variety and scope. It seems that every time I look at another collection or attend another convention, I discover something new. As a very good example, consider the group of dolls depicted on these pages. A very happy group they are—you might say they are having a ball!

Now these dolls are very rare, but still, I cannot think why I had never seen them until last summer. In fact, I must have seen at least a few of them, here and there, during the past 30 years. But I expect that, in my arrogant way (although I protest that I am far from arrogant now), I dismissed them without really looking at them. "Just some more French mignonettes," I must have thought, and those were dolls of which I had long since tired.

Here is another lesson in humility (as if I needed yet another one), for these are French mignonettes with a decided difference. By means of a cunningly simple mechanism, hidden from the casual eye, these little dolls can move. The movement is simple, too—they merely raise and lower their arms—just as the movements of the costly French musical automata are in fact extremely simple. But for both kinds of dolls, their makers have used great imagination in exploiting these movements. When a group of either is collected together, the effect is enchanting.

Not that you are likely to see many groups of hat-tip-

These French mignonettes—whose maker is unknown although some of their heads are marked "F.G."—are called hat-tippers by the author since, by means of a hidden mechanism, they make simple gestures, such as tipping their hats.

Although many of the hat-tippers are courtiers, there are some rustic characters as well, including the two shown above. The gardener offers his garden produce, and the little country maiden throws her apron over her head.

I love these artless little dolls, to whom the secret mechanism imparts such unexpected vitality. But my very favorite is the little country maiden in her pretty peasant dress. She is so shy that, when it is her turn, she throws her apron right over her head!

Maddeningly little is known about these dolls, including why and by whom they were made, although several of the heads on the examples here are marked "F.G." and one little girl is marked "Paris S.L." It is my conjecture that they were intended more as grown-up amusements, rather than specifically as toys for children, just as were the much more expensive musical automata, and the marottes. This helps to explain why so few of them survive, because for such a market, perhaps comparatively few were made.

Back in England, long ago, I owned a very pretty marotte, dressed as Columbine, her skirt and hat encrusted with little bells. She was of that superior kind that has a complete torso, and when she spun to her tinkling music she flung out her arms in a most abandoned way. I had always thought of her as a child's toy, until one day I showed her to a very old lady. "Oh, how nice, a Cotillion favor!" she exclaimed. "I used to love them when I was younger, and I was lucky, I was always winning them!" She explained that at that time, the mid-1870's, the Cotillion was a most popular and energetic dance, the highlight of any ball. It was used as a sort of competition. The music would be stopped at intervals, and the couple nearest to a premarked spot on the dance floor would win, as a prize, just such a marotte.

When I began thinking about the little hat-tippers depicted here, and the luxurious Parisian toy shops where they might have been bought, I remembered that there were also luxurious boutiques, or gift shops as we would call them today. Paris was famous for them. Aladdin's Caves they were, full of lovely little things to give as presents to a lady—fans and perfume and trinkets and gloves and candy boxes and such-like. It is here that the music box automata could be found, together with the Cotillion favors and other frivolities.

I suspect our delightful hat-tippers were to be found in this glamorous company. And I'm sure that more than one proud young English or American lady said to her friends: "Have you seen this charming little toy I've been given? It must have been very expensive—it's French!"

pers comparable to the group described here. These really are very, very rare, and it took their owner more than 25 years of diligent searching to collect 13 of them. I call them hat-tippers because one needs a name, and this polite gesture is a common one among them. A number of the dolls here are dressed as 18th-century courtiers, and these often tip their tricorne hats. Their feminine counterparts raise fans, or lift bouquets to their noses. One of the ladies, in a delicious harlequinade costume, raises her mask while her handsome swain, dressed as a jester, shakes a marotte.

But not all the dolls in this collection are courtiers. There are rustic characters of great charm, including the two splendid horse riders, one of whom tips his hat while his friend waves the American flag. The gardener, mounted somewhat incongruously on a candy box, carries his spade over his shoulder while he offers his garden produce. And a serious little gentleman pursues butterflies with single-minded purpose, his net always at the ready.

To Remember Your Wedding Day

THE AUTHOR TAKES A FOND LOOK AT DOLLS DRESSED, OVER A PERIOD OF 100 YEARS OR SO, AS WEDDING SOUVENIRS

I was only seven years old when I was first taken to a wedding, but I have never forgotten it. Oh, the pleasures of anticipation, to be exceeded only by the wonders of the actuality! As a spectacle, I thought at the time, it must be at least as good as the king's coronation! The year was 1930; it was a glorious June day in London, the peaches-and-cream bride was straight from a fairy tale and the gray, neo-Gothic church was a romantic setting for the fashionable, sweet-pea colors of the bridesmaids—pink, lemon, pale blue, lilac and mint green.

All this was delicious to the eye, and the wedding breakfast that followed was just as delicious to a greedy, young stomach, culminating in the towering, glittering, baroque wedding cake. Vividly memorable to this day is the taste of that cake, rich to blackness, with the curious, scented spiciness of shop-bought confections, a new and exciting taste for me.

But even more memorable was its crowning adornment. This wasn't the usual, trite, bisque figurine of a bridal pair, which I had seen so

often in cake-shop windows. Instead, a pair of dollhouse dolls had been dressed, with great panache, in black and cream satins and a little cloud of tulle, to make a commendable replica of the wedding couple themselves. I remember that a great deal was made of these bridal dolls and the lady who made them was congratulated

On the top of Mrs. Ray Hulet's wedding cake, in the mid 1920's, was this pair of wedding dolls. The groom is a bisque-headed dollhouse doll and the bride is a half-doll with fixed arms and a wire-supported hoop skirt.

The china head shown at right is dressed in material from the wedding dress of Sarah Underhill, a Quaker from Philadelphia. The detail of Sarah Underhill's china head, above, hints at her unusual coiffure.

bility of sentiment!

Some years ago, the Museum of the City of New York received as a gift just such a pair of wedding-cake dolls as I saw in my childhood. They were the gift of Mrs. Ray Hulet and they had been on the top of her own wedding cake in the mid 1920's—a trifle earlier, perhaps, than the ones I remember, but in much the same genre. Indeed, the bridegroom is exactly the same bisque-headed dollhouse doll that I remember. But Hulet's is an amusingly mismatched pair and her bride is a pretty half-doll with fixed arms of the sort intended to be made up as pincushions, her hoop skirt supported by a wire cage.

The black-and-cream-clad dolls from my childhood were very smart indeed, and I fancy that today we would label them Art Deco. But Hulet's dolls were conceived very romantically in what could be called the "Hollywood Louis XVI" manner. Their satins and silks are all ivory colored, and they are much ruffled with lace. A close inspection will uncover fragments of icing sugar, still clinging both to the hem of the bride's gown and to the bridegroom's shoes—this, I feel, is a truly romantic touch!

My second example of a wedding souvenir is also to be found in the Museum of the City of New York. It is a ravishingly lovely, glazed china-head doll with its black, painted hair arranged in an unusual coiffure, dressed back in rippling waves from a center part to a braided coronet,

over and again. "Ah, well," she said modestly, although beaming with gratified pride, "I wanted the bride to have something different, something really nice for a souvenir."

We English are a sentimental brood, and so, I have found, are many Americans, and since at least the early 19th century, we have all been happily cluttering our lives and our homes with souvenirs of all kinds, from our first baby shoes and our christening mug to the engraved watch or mantel clock presented on our retirement. And it seems that there is a tradition, so much a part of us as not really to be recognized as such, for remembering a wedding day with a pair of souvenir dolls. In choosing examples for this article, I was amused to see that between the earliest and latest there is a span of more than 100 years—demonstrating clearly, if proof were really needed, the dura-

at the heart of which is modeled a tall, curving tuck comb. This rare feature is enough to rate a star in any collection. But for this particular doll, beauty is only part of its attraction, for it comes with a fascinating history. It was the unlikely choice of a celebrated Quaker lady, Sarah Underhill, as the doll to be dressed by her as a souvenir of her wedding, in fragments of her own wedding dress.

Underhill was a Quaker from Philadelphia who

came to live in New York after her marriage. She became well known during the 1860's for her active, indeed, pioneering work for various neglected human causes. She appears to have been intelligent and businesslike, and her granddaughter, Lydia LeBaron Walker, the donor of the doll, remembers that her one recorded vanity was the fresh, pink, hundred-petal rose which she always wore at her bosom on formal occasions. The doll is wearing just such a rose at the bosom of its fine silk dress. The cut of this garment is plain, as one would expect, and so is the matching "Quaker" bonnet but the fabric is luxurious and is of the beautiful almond-green color associated with Quaker ladies. Looking at this lovely doll, so carefully kept for over a century, one can safely assume that even if Sarah Underhill had so little vanity, she was by no means without sentiment.

Our third wedding souvenir doll is decidedly sentimental and has all the added charm of the miniature, being barely four inches tall. It has no known history, although it is presumed to have come from England. It is a little

It seems to me that there is a tradition, so much a part of us that we do not recognize it as one, for remembering a wedding day with a pair of souvenir dolls.

wooden doll from the Grodner Tal and it has been charmingly and most stylishly dressed in the fashion of 1830. The wide sleeves and pantaloons are made from a close-textured blue silk but the skirt, the double bertha and the little poke bonnet are contrived from parchment and decorated with blue beads (something blue?) and grains of rice, which may be the very ones thrown at this Biedermeier bride. The beads are smaller and finer than anything obtainable today. The rich effect is heightened by borders of multi-colored beads, mixed with white.

The doll lies complacently in a bed of cambric flowers—rose leaves and lilac sprays, faded now to palest ivory, but undoubtedly once the ornament of a wedding dress. This little treasure is preserved under a small, shallow glass dome, its black base reeded, as is proper for a "shade" of this date.

My last example is the earliest, and, very suitably, the rarest. It is a pair of early, German, papier-mâché-headed dolls of the kind still known by the erroneous title Milliner's Models. This ridiculous misnomer survives, perhaps because it rolls so trippingly off the tongue, and certainly because no one has yet invented a better, truer name!

These dolls are nine inches high, and are dressed as a wedding couple. They were found in rural Pennsylvania and they have a sunny, pastoral appearance that I find quite enchanting. They also have great simplicity and one would assume that the bride and groom whom they record were Plain People from one of the less stringent sects. Or perhaps they, too, were Quakers? I cannot tell since the minute knowledge of local Protestant customs necessary to identify a wedding couple from so long ago and faraway is not easily come by. I say long ago, because the dress of this bride cannot be later than

Four inches high, this wedding doll is a wooden Grodner Tal, probably from England. Dressed in the style of 1830, she's surrounded by faded rose leaves and lilac sprays that probably decorated the original owner's bridal gown.

1810 and might be as much as a decade earlier. Her groom's long coat and wide-brimmed hat support this dating.

All this is delightful enough, but my special joy in this happy pair lies in the fact that their clothes have been contrived, with skill and considerable style, entirely from corn husks. This would be a masterly achievement at any date but here it gives to the dolls great added importance, since it makes this pair by far the earliest examples of corn husk dolls that I can remember. There was, of course, a rage for them in the 1880's and 1890's, and many lovely corn husk dolls have been preserved for us from that era. The beautiful pair at The Mary Merritt Doll Museum in Douglassville, Pennsylvania, comes at once to mind—and they too, oddly enough, are wedding souvenir dolls. But the ones illustrated here, made at least 70 years earlier, are to the best of my knowledge, unique.

They stand to return our gaze, gravely enough, and at first we don't notice the pretty, fanciful details of their clothes—the corn-silk hair, worn by both dolls at shoulder length; his coat buttons, charmingly contrived, like her brooch, from seeds; the wreaths of seed stalks representing flowers, which adorn both her bonnet and his hat (the latter reminding me irresistibly of the romantic wreaths of roses and wild flowers that used to be worn around straw hats by Eton College boys on Boating Day).

Instead of a bouquet, our bride has a modest basket of flowers, while her groom carries, rolled up and tucked handily into his coat pocket, their marriage certificate. This charming pair is so fresh and neat that I feel sure they were only plucked recently from the glass case that must have protected them for more than 170 years. They are kept safely behind glass now and away from direct light, too, and one day shall have a case of their own restored to them, with a setting of dried leaves and grasses, like the ones at The Mary Merritt.

I know of few other collectors who delight in these souvenir dolls but I should like very much to hear from

Often called, inappropriately, Milliner's Models, these two nine-inch-high, early, German, papier-mâché-headed dolls are dressed in corn-husk wedding clothes. Owned by the author, they were found in rural Pennsylvania and are thought to represent a Mennonite or Quaker couple. The bride's dress, done in the style of the early 1800's, is accessorized with a seed brooch; the groom's coat is closed with seed buttons. Both have seed-stalk flowers adorning their hats.

those who do and to become acquainted with their treasures, especially with other early examples. The last three dolls described and depicted here are from my own collection and I have the nicest memories of acquiring them and of the good friends who made their acquisition possible. My pleasure in contemplating these old wedding souvenirs is doubled when they are also, for me, souvenirs of friendship.

The Bagmen's Babies

The origins of these quaint 18th-century dolls are still a mystery

Thirty years ago, very little was known about the antique dolls which were being collected so avidly. The few books about dolls available at the time had been compiled by enthusiastic amateurs, and while the books are invaluable in that they record facts (as well as hearsay) and many interesting examples which have since disappeared, there was, alas, not one author among these who was a professional researcher. We had to wait for Dorothy Coleman's daughters, still in high school, to grow a little older, and for the famous trio to become interested in old dolls and focus their awesome talents upon them, before true and indisputable knowledge was set out before us.

"We know so little, so very little!" I can remember Dorothy lamenting in her soft, Washington accent, and by "we" she did not refer to the Colemans and myself, but to the doll world as a whole. Gentle she might be, but Dorothy had a strength of purpose, coupled with a deep love for the art of research—for an art it undoubtedly is, as well as a science—which kept that focus steady for the next three decades, to produce the staggering encyclopedias which have become the doll collector's bibles.

The Colemans were the leaders, but since their spearhead, I am delighted to observe that others—well-informed and professional researchers—both here and in Europe, have focused their own spotlights on the dolls that they love. From being "just a hobby for little old ladies in tennis shoes," as one of my museum directors witheringly described my life-long passion, dolls have become one of the best-researched

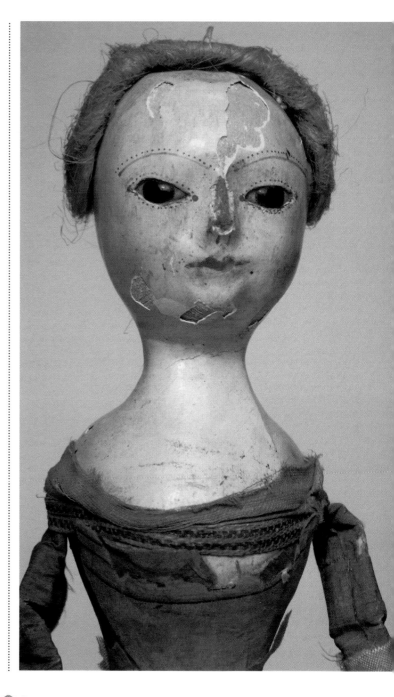

The 11-inch-high wooden at right and on the following page, circa 1840, has inset glass eyes, tow hair and her original dress, made of vertical stripes of silk over a paper lining. She was donated to the Museum of the City of New York by Sophia L. McDonald.

areas in the antiques field.

With all this, it is surprising that there are still groups of dolls about which very little is known, which stand on our shelves contained and silent, keeping their histories and purposes to themselves. For me at least, such dolls positively glitter with romance and mystery. The scandalous French "court" dolls comprise one such group—and very sinister and delicious they are. And perhaps, one day, a clue will surface—a letter, a document, a painting, perhaps—which will explain them.

Another group of 18th-century dolls are equally reserved about their origins, although they have been with us from the beginning of the collecting hobby. We know of no proper name for them, and such understanding of them as we have is from informed conjecture, as historians would put it. In calling them "bagmen's dolls," I am in the company of such illustrious, informed collectors as Mary Hillier, but the name is still conjecture, and should properly be used with quotation marks.

I refer, of course, to the enchantingly stylized wooden dolls, with their hands like wooden forks, their sloe-black eyes and hair of plaited tow. Their costumes, simplified to a uniform, feature the wide panniers which were at the height of their popularity in the · 1730's. However, these dolls, as we know from documentation, were made in exactly the same way for a number of decades, long after such panniers had gone from the fashionable scene and were only worn at court.

A second striking feature of these dolls is that their dresses are always made from a kind of vertical, silk patchwork, usually comprised of several weights of fabric, from heavy brocade to plain rep, to the thinnest silken lining fabric. The effect is always very rich. Most of the dresses are ornamented, albeit very simply, with a woven braid striped with silver thread, adding a note of sumptuousness that is enhanced by the fact that the dresses have been made very long—half as long again as the doll itself, whose sketchy little legs dangle inside the great envelope of the skirt.

The skirts are always lined with heavy paper, and the necklaces of glass beads that sometimes survive, I believe, may have been original. But I suspect that the other delightful accessories with which we can find some examples endowed—hats and calashes, shawls, jackets, fans or canes and, in the case of one splendid beauty, a silver spoon hanging on a chain from her neck—I fear, have been added, hopefully by the doll's first owner after it had been purchased. I say this

because, unlike the superior dolls of this period, which had individual attention lavished on them from their inception—which were, if I may use a modern phrase, "entirely custom-made"—our "bagmen's babies" are thoroughly commercial products, turned out in quantity and as quickly as possible, and sold in bulk, perhaps by the bagmen, the itinerant tradesmen of that time.

It was in a book entitled *English Dolls, Effigies and Puppets*, written by an English collector, Alice K. Early, and published in 1955, that I first encountered the following fascinating piece of evidence, concerning dollmaking in the first half of the 18th century. It is an extract from *The Sessions of Peace*, April 1733 (alas, in her charming, amateurish way, Early did not bother to tell us where these sessions were held, but one presumes a country town). Joseph Phips and Jane Tinsley, who seem to have been apprentice and house servant respectively, were indicted for stealing "14 naked babies [dolls] and 2 dozen of dressed babies, and one jointed baby," the goods of Williams Higgs.

At the session Higgs states: "I am a turner by trade [this means he would have made furniture, especially chairs, with legs, etc. turned on a lathe] but my chief business is to make babies, and when they are made my wife dresses them; my boy and journeywoman followed the same sort of work."

Suspecting the theft, Higgs's wife went to the maid's lodging and found there one of Higgs's "matted chairs," which the landlady protested she had bought honestly from the apprentice. Upon this, Higgs got a search warrant, and found 14 of his own dolls hidden in the maid's room. "I know my own babies from any other man's, I can swear to my own work, for there's never another man in England that makes such babies, besides myself."

More of his missing dolls were found at the house of Johanna Morgan. Two dozen dressed babies lay in a basket—ready, presumably, to be taken out to sell "to a man in St. Catherine's Lane, that has bespoke them." Happily, the prisoners were acquitted, although the blame seems to have fallen on "Nell-What-do-you-call-her, a crooked body" (compared to Jane Tinsley, who is described as "a very honest body"). We are not told of Nell's fate in this extract, and I am left apprehensive, since the punishments for such petty thefts as this were alarmingly harsh, and Nell, if convicted, may even have been hanged.

This one vivid little insight tells us a great deal

This doll from the author's collection gains dignity from her memorial case, where she is framed in a garland of 18th-century fish-scale flowers, although these are later additions. The bodice of this doll's dress is beautifully fashioned.

about dollmaking in England in the early-18th century. These wooden dolls, all of which were lathe-turned and then refined by hand, were made as a sideline by the turner or furniture maker. His wife dressed them, surely in scraps of the upholstery materials, since Higgs could put very little money into toys, which he sold for 15 shillings for half a gross, or twopence halfpenny each. Thus we can see that Higg's little factory, which he described so proudly, was in fact a sweatshop, with everybody in it working hard to produce the stream of dolls, which had been sold in bulk, to provide a very modest existence.

We have, alas, no more evidence about Higgs, but his story certainly fits with our so-called "bagmen's babies," so obviously mass-produced, following a tradition, as did Higgs's "other men who make babies, besides myself." The overlong, panniered, paper-lined skirt, whipped up by the dozen from the patchwork strips of leftover upholstery material, was an easy way to give substance and importance to the trivial little dolls. A few simple skills needed, exercised for long hours, every day, would result in a crisp, neat product.

Such handsome toys, produced by lowly and uneducated craftspeople, may surely claim to be folk art, a term too casually used these days. And perhaps, one day soon, one of our indefatigable researchers will find even more first-hand evidence to illuminate these fascinating, if mysterious, toys of two centuries ago.

Plain & Fancy Handiwork

THE CAREFUL SEWING THAT LITTLE GIRLS WERE TAUGHT IN THE 19TH CENTURY PRODUCED HOMEMADE CLOTH DOLLS OF ALL KINDS—SOME CRUDE, SOME EXQUISITE, BUT ALL ENDEARING TO PRESENT-DAY COLLECTORS

W hat is your favorite kind of doll?" This is one of the questions that is often put to me when I meet a group of collectors, and it is a question that I find very difficult to answer, since I have so many favorite kinds. All I can say then, to excuse myself, is "early ones!" And that is certainly true. But high up on my list of favorites, of any period, are the dolls that are handmade, that bear the clear immediate impact of their maker's personality. This, of course, is why I am so delighted with today's artist dolls and why I am so very fond of old handmade cloth dolls, especially those humble ones that were made at home, by craftsmen with perhaps more love than skill.

·I am not familiar with the curricula of modern-day schools, but I imagine that plain and fancy needlework no longer figures among the daily lessons of little American girls. When I myself was at school in England in the mid-1920's, such sewing lessons formed an important part of a little girl's education. Every afternoon, in our "Junior Mixed" classroom (for ages eight to eleven) we boys would be given some simple form of handiwork to do—constructions in cardboard, perhaps, model-making, and so on—while the girls opened their sewing bags and spent the next hour hemming and French-seaming under the teacher's watchful eyes. From Monday to Wednesday the girls were taught the elements of plain sewing, and at the end of term could take home handkerchiefs and pajama cases, and eventually pinafores and petticoats, as proof of their skill and industry. But on Thursday and Friday, their fancywork was produced from

The engraving from the *American Girl's Book*, top, shows a mother teaching her daughters to sew. The girls above are barely three inches high and, from the stylish dresses, can be dated to the 1860's or early 1870's.

itation of fingers; therefore, all you can do is to round off the hands in as shapely a manner as possible.

Next cut out two pieces of linen for the back and front of the doll's body, and give the waist a handsome tapering shape. Afterwards cut out the legs from the hips to the knees; and then, in two separate pieces, the legs from the knees to the ancles; shaping them well. Lastly, cut out the feet in four pieces, two for each side.

All these different parts of the doll must be sewed separately, stuffed tightly with bran, and then strongly sewed up at the ends. They must be stuffed so hard that they cannot be dented.

AMERICAN GIRL'S BOOK.

A JOINTED LINEN DOLL.

Linen dolls, when large and properly y afford more pleasure to little childrer wax, wood, or composition, as they can played with freely; and, when soiled ily repaired. No child can hurt its

AMERICAN GIRL'S BOOK. 306

A COMMON LINEN DOLL.

These dolls are easily made, and answer every purpose for very small children. They may be of any size, from a quarter of a yard long to a finger's length. Some little girls make a dozen of these dolls together and play at school with them.

These book pages are from the *American Girl's Book*, first published in Massachusetts in 1831, and give instructions for making linen dolls.

In the early children's books the little girl is exhorted to ply her needle, or is praised for the skill with which she has made her dolls' clothing.

la. Children from London now found themselves in country village schools where, for the girls, gardening and cooking lessons were of urgent, national importance, while the boys alternately learned farming skills from their teachers and defense techniques from the local Home Guard Corps, for this was a time when the threat of invasion was real and immediate. So ended a tradition that reached back through the centuries to the Middle Ages and beyond. Instruction for schoolgirls in the ancient, womanly arts of the needle on the old, daily basis were never resumed.

Throughout those centuries, a proficiency in sewing was a necessary thing, when all clothing, bedding and soft furnishing, except for those of the very well-to-do, had to be made at home. And even in aristocratic houses, the ladies spent their long, leisurely days with sewing needles in their hands, producing exquisite, embroidered luxury items such as caps, purses and pockets, bodices, whole dresses and petticoats, besides all sorts of similar garments for their menfolk. With the help of an army of female servants, they produced needleworked bedcovers and bed hangings, curtains and tablecloths and even the yardage for upholstered furniture, on a scale and of such splendor as to be

those capacious bags, and they bent their heads over crewels and silks, over drawn-thread work, which often drew tears, or crochet and beadwork, which they all seemed to enjoy.

Such instruction went on all over England, in what Americans would call the public schools, until the outbreak of the Second World War, when the mass evacuations of school children made chaos of the old curricu-

mind-boggling—at least to the 20th-century mind.

All this is surely of great interest to doll collectors, since it accounts for the enchantingly beautiful and intricate clothing to be found on many of the earliest dolls. The elaborate corsetry, the fontanges and embroidered caps, the dresses with their panniers and saque backs, the quilted petticoats—all this may have been the work of skilled ladies' maids, but it may very well have been achieved by the young owner of the doll herself. Dressing her doll could well have been one more exercise in the sewing arts, which by that time were desirable accomplishments for young ladies.

When we come to the 19th century, this desirability is more clearly defined and acknowledged. The rise of the middle classes had set a premium on gentility as early as 1810, when we first began to get books printed especially for children. Very stiff and moral in tone they were, alas, and over and over the little girl is exhorted to ply her needle, or is praised for the skill with which she has made her dolls' clothing. Again, if we look with this circumstance in mind, we can find many dolls of this period whose delicate dresses of white muslin and embroidered cambric may well have been the work of their young owner.

The first quarter of the 19th century saw the birth and circulation of monthly "ladies' magazines," and although these were at first painfully genteel, assuming that their readers had never entered a kitchen or seen a spade, by the 1850's they had found a wider market and had proliferated, and were clearly aimed at a middle-class readership. And it is in these mid-century magazines that we begin to find fascinating instructions for the making and dressing of cloth dolls.

No one, to my knowledge, has as yet researched and cataloged the many such magazines published at this time in England, Europe and America. This study, I imagine, would merit a master's degree, and should any ambitious student embark on it, I should be thrilled and eager to know. Such a project could be taken a fascinating step further, and having found the instructions for particular cloth dolls, the researcher could then look for actual, made-up specimens. Several such dolls are the

A glance at Lord Cedric's clothing dates him to between 1820 and 1830. He has the look of a country gentleman whose life is centered around his estate and the welfare of his herds and crops.

subject of this article, and here the research could be done in reverse, for our dolls all have great personality and originated, most likely, from instructions in ladies' magazines.

This group probably dates from the early 1860's. It has a direct and primitive quality. The gentleman on the left is shown in detail on the opposite page.

The dolls featured here are all from the same collection, that of my dear friend, Winnie Langley. Winnie has always cherished a special love for cloth dolls and, like myself, she is most fond of the unusual, perhaps one-of-a-kind handmade dolls, about which little or nothing is known, dolls that are a delight to the eye and a challenge to the mind.

The doll on the preceding page is one that is very close to Winnie's heart. He is called Lord Cedric, and while his origin is a mystery, a glance at his clothing will tell us that this is a very early doll, made, I would venture, between 1820 and 1830. His suit has

"trowsers," which were very new and smart at that time, and his jacket is distinguished by its very sloping shoulders and exceedingly high collar. His shirt collar has the high points which were so uncomfortable and so difficult to maintain, and they are set off by a blue-satin cravat. His velvet hat has a very wide brim, which has become much creased and worn over the years. Originally it must have been firm and straight. It is lined with silk, and has a double band of ribbon. It surely represented a practical beaver hat to be worn in the country. And this, to my mind, defines Lord Cedric's social position. Besides his decidedly aristocratic bearing, he has a rustic look, the look of a country gentleman whose life is centered around his estate and the welfare of his herds and crops.

The next group of three dolls is much later, at least from the mid 19th century. From the lady's dress and the gentleman's bold checked "trowsers," I should hazard a date somewhere in the early 1860's. Like all the other dolls discussed here, their origin is a mystery, but from the sturdy nature of the men's clothing, I should imagine that these dolls are from a Northern climate. However this may be, the direct and primitive quality of this trio has produced an enchanting, vibrant look entirely their own. Their personalities are so vivid that they almost speak. One longs to play with them.

I have saved the best until last, hugging the delight of them to myself, as indeed, I wish heartily that I could

Among the projects in the *American Girl's Book* were instructions for making this black doll.

do. Since I first began to collect dolls, when I was still a child, I have tried to avoid envy and jealousy, since these emotions can destroy all the pleasure that these old playthings can offer. Such good resolves weaken, alarmingly, when one is confronted with dolls so delicious, so utterly covetable, as those that comprise our last example. But how lucky I am that they should belong to Winnie, who lives barely a mile away, so that I can see these darlings whenever I visit her.

To begin with, this little group is very small, barely three inches high, and they are kept safely within a miniature frame, the sort with a convex glass. Again, nothing is known of them, but from the stylish dresses, I should place them in the 1860's or early 1870's. Two little girls, surely in their Sunday best, are swinging a smaller child in their arms, and the group is fixed, sewn firmly together. The tiny faces are modeled with the needle, with minute, applied noses, the other features defined with infinitesimal stitchery. The child's hands

and all the details of the pretty clothing are perfect. The color is limpid and delicate, and the whole group retains a dewy freshness, as though the last stitches had been sewn yesterday.

This little group, so sophisticated and elegant, is in sharp contrast to the rusticity of Lord Cedric and, together with the lively family, they demonstrate the wide variety of unpretentious, handmade cloth dolls that survives to us from the past. They were made mostly at home, by those little girls grown up, who were taught needlework as a matter of course. Whether competently sculpted or endearingly primitive, they all show this womanly skill, at the time so universal.

There are still wonderful cloth dolls being made today, but no longer in every other home. Today's doll artists are a breed apart, dedicated and brilliant, but their beautiful dolls are now a valid art form. I myself delight in them, although I look back with regret to the days when every housewife could sew and most of them made enchanting dolls for their little girls, who themselves were industriously acquiring the ancient, magical skills with the needle.

Sewing Companions

THE AUTHOR TAKES A FOND LOOK AT SOME FRIVOLOUS
TOYS USED BY VICTORIAN LADIES AT THEIR WORK

I n an earlier article, I looked at some of the cloth dolls made at home by the mothers and sisters of Victorian children, and I commented rather sadly on the fact that such skills with the needle—either plain or fancy—are no longer taught, as a matter of course, in our schools. Since setting down my thoughts on this subject, I have been pondering further—why, I wonder, do these traditional skills seem quite unnecessary in this day and age?

True, this is a faster-paced world that we now live in. Women are much more active, and in this throwaway, disposable culture, there is perhaps no practical necessity for sewing skills. When did I last meet a person who darns stockings, turns sheets to middle or embroiders blouses?

But in the 19th century, and for most of the first half of this one, fine sewing was an accomplishment in which young girls took pride. These skills were used by them as an allurement for young men, whose offers of marriage were all-important in an age when, for most women—even the best-educated—domesticity was the only possible career.

Then, the drawing room or the parlor was the ladies' daily setting. (Who today has a room in their house called by either name and serving this function?) There, wearing pretty dresses suitable for the afternoon or the evening, the daughters of the house sat with their mother. As they stitched away—interminably, it would seem to us—at their Berlinwork or their Italian quilting, making cushion covers or lacy caps or frivolous trifles for the church bazaar, they were aware, of course, that they appeared to great advantage at these decorative tasks, just as they did when they sat at the piano or the harp to play their parlor pieces, and to sing their drawing-room ballads.

I once read a particularly colorful Victorian novel, and although I cannot recall the author, one striking passage has stayed in my mind: "She appeared like Circe, weaving enchantments, as with pretty, pale fingers she plied her needle." And in a description of a

AMERICAN GIRL'S BOOK.

272

RETICULES.

A DOLL BAG.

Get a doll's head, of composition. Make a square bag out of a quarter of a yard of silk, and run a case for a drawing-string at the top. Sew the shoulders of the

showed them off to advantage. And to aid her in her endeavors, there were all kinds of pretty sewing equipment to enchant the eye still further. Every young lady owned a sewing box, of course, usually a present from her parents, and as handsome as they could afford. But she also had all kinds of novel sewing aids, or sewing companions, as they were known, with which to amuse herself.

The first sewing companion that we present here is early, from about 1830, and it is quite tiny, measuring barely four inches in any direction (**figure 1**). On a dark, printed silk-velvet rug stands a homemade wing chair, covered with rich blue silk. A tiny wooden Grodner Tal lady sits in its depths. She is dressed in lavender silk with a lace apron. She knits on two straight pins, and carries a

Berlinwool picture of the 1860's, worked simultaneously by a young lady and her mother, Beverly Nichols noted that one passage of a sheep's coat was clumsier than all the rest—"As though, perhaps, Walter had been watching their hands as they worked, and had taken advantage of her mother's brief absence to capture the available needle, and put in some stitches with a hand much less skilled, but very much more exciting."

I suspect that these are clues to the primary reasons why the cultivation of needle skills has languished, for in these sophisticated days, a woman does not need to "catch a man." But then they did their best, and their best must have been enchanting to behold. Their clothes and manners were beautiful and unworldly, and evoked for their admirers the illusion of a mysterious, blissful world set apart—the woman's world, the haven of the helpmeet, to which the militant male could turn after the hurly-burly of breadwinning—a concept that today has entirely vanished from our society.

There she sat in her mother's parlor, the daughter of the house, decorous and, she hoped, desirable, demurely sewing away, aware that her hands were white and elegant, and that their movements among the threads

1850's, and the doll is a so-called milliner's model. Her blue-and-black, slightly military costume includes a shako-like hat that encompasses a pincushion; and another pincushion hangs from her waist. Pockets on her full, blue skirt are shaped to hold packets of fine needles, while beneath it, a bunchy, starched petticoat has capacious pockets that are closed with drawstrings, and appear to be full of buttons.

To one side of her skirt is sewn a silk bucket-like container that holds a silver thimble. At her back, slung there by ribbons, is another, larger pack that accommodates a long paper of darning needles, a steel crochet hook and a pair of steel scissors.

The colored, engraved illustration of a similar doll, viewed from front and back and brave with scarlet wool, was issued in a mid-century copy of *Peterson's Magazine* (**figure 5**). A few lucky collectors have found dolls that Victorian readers dressed, following this pattern exactly.

Popular some ten years later were dolls dressed like our third example, seen on the right in **figure 3**. This beautiful Parian has been most fetchingly attired in a military costume. It smacks of the uniform of the French Zouaves, and is associated with the heroine of the story that became an opera, and then was immortalized by the legendary Jenny Lind. The Daughter of the Regiment is

minute silk reticule over her arm. A larger green silk reticule, or sewing bag, is pinned to the arm of her chair. An even tinier, similar wooden doll sits before her on a red satin pincushion, next to a most exquisitely made sewing basket, with hand-painted silk panels. The basket contains two elaborate silver and gold thimbles, one set around with corals.

A young ladies' book of the 1830's contains directions for constructing two such sewing companion dolls (**figure 2**). One is described as a reticule, and the instructions for making it explain that it is in fact a sewing bag, disguised as a doll, while the other is a doll, dressed to hold everyday sewing equipment. These are unusually early examples.

Not quite so early is our second companion, seen at left in **figure 3**, above, with a rear view in **figure 4, on the opposite page**. This one dates from the late 1840's or early

WORK TABLE COMPANION,
For the Lady's Friend.

commemorated by many dolls of the period. Here again, the doll carries a thimble in what might otherwise be a waterskin, the drum by her side is a useful box, and the pack on her back is an efficient needlecase.

I have spoken of the ubiquitous workboxes, the elegance of their finish and the neat disposal of their contents. Our last example here is what must surely be the penultimate sewing box—a box such as only a very well-established young lady might aspire to (**figures 6** and **7**). It dates from the late 1860's.

This box is a deep oblong, and is made of a rare and luxuriously figured satinwood, the top banded with ebony and with a string of inlaid work. It opens ponderously and smoothly, to reveal an elaborate interior, lined with deep-blue paper and quilted satin of a paler blue, all edged and bordered with gilt and silver braids and with crimped lace. The box is fitted with

perfume bottles, a pincushion and spools in their own nests, while a hinged holder accommodates a needle case, scissors, awl and thimble, all matching, and all rich with gilt, embossing and enamel.

The lid is recessed to form a little stage, backed with a mirror, and here sits a little bisque doll, in profile. It represents a tailor, fantastically dressed in colored satins, with gilt "Dresden" paper trimmings. The turn of the key and the flick of a switch set a music box in motion, and the tailor sews industriously at his length of lawn, to the tinkling tune.

How charming it must have been to watch the young lady stitching, with this delicious companion at her side. How like Circe she must have seemed indeed, weaving her delicate enchantments to the frail, fairytale music, as with pretty, pale fingers she plied her sweet needle. I can picture her clearly, and sigh for the loss of such subtle delights.

What's In a Name?

THE AUTHOR PONDERS HIS BELOVED ENGLISH WAXES

I n a recent issue, I left my readers contemplating, among other delights, the lovely marked Montanari that was among the first few dolls to come into my life. I took us back some 40 years to war-wracked London, where in the daytime the skies were peppered with barrage balloons, while the nighttime skies were made hideous with anti-aircraft gunfire. I was barely 21, and I was teaching arts and crafts in a prestigious private school. I had already made a collection of all kinds of small antiques and "bygones"—Staffordshire figures, for instance, and Japanese netsukes, valentines and Victorian children's books, and much more besides. As a schoolboy I used to save up most of my pocket money to squander on these collections, and I loved them. But most of all I loved my old toys, and especially my old dollhouses and my old dolls.

In those days, there were almost no other collectors of such things, and no published information about old dolls, at least none available to me. It was to be years before I was introduced to the books of Henry-René D'Allemagne, of Karl Grober and Max von Boehn, and the writings of the elegant and aristocratic Mrs. Neville Jackson. And even had I found their books, these collectors had written them nearly half a century before, and about dolls from an even more remote past.

I was in fact enormously lucky, I now realize, to be an innocent in this mysterious, uncharted paradise of toys, where every new find, every fresh old doll looked at with my innocent eyes could open up a rich field for speculation and wonder, unsullied by other people's conjectures and judgments. I knew enough to recognize the signature of my Montanari doll, although I cannot now remember just how I knew—perhaps it was information gleaned from one of the two other collectors that I had met as a I scoured the street markets: the intrepid Irene Blair Hickman or the indefatigable Laura Tresko. Perhaps, although both these ladies were very protective of their knowledge.

It was not until late in the 1940s, after the war had ended, that I found in my public library a copy of *Dolls of*

Figure 1: Anne Elizabeth Holden as she looks today; she is one of the lovely wax dolls in the collection of Dorothy Dixon.

Figure 2: The page from Alice K. Early's book, *English Dolls, Effigies and Puppets*, showing the wax doll, Anne Elizabeth Holden, as she looked in 1956.

Three Centuries, by Eleanor St. George. What a red-letter day that was! I turned the pages with impatient fingers, and read the text with amazement, for across the Atlantic there seemed to be a whole organized society of doll collectors, gathering up dolls such as I had never heard of before. All at once, how small my own little collection seemed, and how insignificant my own dolls became by comparison.

Eleanor St. George was clearly a lady of some substance, not to say social standing, and she introduced me to the early German peg woodens and papier-mâchés; she

presented to my dazzled eyes the glories of French bisques and of German parians; and through her pages I learned of the marvelous cloth dolls made—in Victorian New England—by a remarkable woman called Izannah Walker. Mrs. St. George, in her forthright, Yankee way, was very free with her opinions and judgments, which I accepted as gospel, being far too ignorant to question them. Mrs. St. George's writing was indeed powerful, heady stuff, and for me, this Yankee lady created an American dream world, a never-never land, where one could form close friendships with other collectors a thousand miles away, and where a French lady doll could be exchanged for a pressure cooker. At that time, I had never even heard of a pressure cooker, and the world of American doll collectors seemed to me as remote and exotic as Xanadu. It was not until 1956 that a book was published by an English collector, in the pages of which I felt thoroughly at home.

The book was *English Dolls, Effigies and Puppets*, and the author was an Englishwoman, Alice K. Early. Mrs. Early was clearly a lady of good family, and she too was a woman of substance. But

Figure 3: At left is another lovely wax doll, unmarked but most probably a Montanari; she is from Dorothy Dixon's collection. Figure 4: Above is Alice K. Early's illustration, found opposite page 114 in her book, of her so-called "granny" doll.

she was writing from my home ground, in a curiously gentle and recessive manner that I found very reassuring. She was obviously well educated, and her text was carefully, although amateurishly, researched. This was endearing and sometimes maddening, as when Mrs. Early quoted without listing her sources, or when she recorded oral traditions—always most valuable, except that she neglected to tell us whose traditions they were.

Nevertheless, for me her book was epoch-making, and the lovely dolls depicted in generous numbers within her pages were of kinds familiar and dear to me. There were particularly beautiful and desirable English wax dolls, especially a Montanari, to be found opposite page 110. The description of this beauty, shown in **figure 2**, was disappointingly brief: "Another Montanari doll has fair hair

Figure 5: The doll shown in figure 4 as she looks today, clad in a simple white dress and bonnet. She is marked: "To be had of E. Tinker, 54 Bishopsgate, and no where else." She is from the collection of Winnie Langley.

and real eyebrows. She belonged to the daughter of the first Lord Holden, and is beautifully dressed and shod. Her gown is of blue to match her dark blue eyes. For evening she is décolleté, and wears a flowery-lace cap. For day wear she adds sleeves and a fringed scarf, and wears a quilted silk bonnet."

It can be imagined how I pored over those rather foggy photographs, and how puzzled I was, for this beautiful doll, Anne Elizabeth Holden, which I now know to be quite characteristic of the earliest Montanaris, was not at all like my own marked one. It was some years before it dawned on me that my doll was almost certainly made later, by Richard rather than his mother, Augusta Montanari.

My regular readers will know that I moved a few years ago to California, and that I am lucky enough to live less than a mile from my good friends, Dorothy Dixon and Winnie Langley, and their legendary collections of dolls. It was during one of my first visits to them that Dorothy placed a wax doll in my arms, and I found myself gazing at Anne Elizabeth Holden, shown as she looks today in **figure 1**.

Again, you can imagine my joy, to be followed shortly by bewilderment, when it transpired that this doll, for years my measure for a Montanari, is not marked in any way. Perhaps Mrs. Early had positive proof of the doll's manufacture, but if so, she did not pass it on to us.

Another lovely wax doll in Dorothy Dixon's collection may be noted here, for it too is an unmarked wax with the characteristics of a Montanari, as may be seen from her picture, **figure 3**. Although this is a child doll, it is dressed in a baby's long robe, and this is not unusual, for from the

mid-Victorian period, dolls clearly representing children or even adults are to be found dressed in baby clothes.

A doll from Mrs. Early's book is in Winnie Langley's collection, too, and a very remarkable doll it is. Its photograph, **figure 4**, is found in the book opposite page 114, and the following description is on page 115: "About the same period (c. 1800) is a doll who has a fine muslin cap over her gray curls, and her head and shoulders, arms and feet are of wax, and her body of firmly stuffed calico. Her chemise and petticoats and gown are of very fine piqué, and her overdress is of fine purple gauze, with silk braid fitting it tightly to the bosom. She has a high frill round the décolletage. Her date is c. 1805. Whereas nearly all dolls insist on being young and beautiful, this doll has the distinction of being an old lady."

In 1956 I did not question Mrs. Early's last statement, although this seemed to me to be a decidedly odd and even inexplicable doll. But since then, I have seen quite a number of wax dolls of this period sporting gray hair, and they cannot all have been intended to represent grannies. The answer can be found, I think, in the fashion plates of the day, or of a slightly earlier date. I am thinking especially of the splendid prints from *Heideloff's Gallery of Fashion*, that glorious publication that appeared, under Royal patronage, throughout most of the 1790s and the early 1800s.

If we examine the volumes from the mid 1790s—1795, let us say—we find that almost all the elegant ladies who model the clothes have gray, powdered hair, and this charming style was worn no matter what time of day. We can see it affected, too, by the aristocratic ladies in fashionable portraits of the time, painted by Gainsborough or Reynolds—ladies strolling in their grounds or seated upon their horses, all with gray, powdered hair. Oddly enough, a late 18th-century wax doll, with just such a powdered coiffure, is pictured right there in Mrs. Early's book, opposite page 132. I am surprised that she did not make the connection.

Such a highborn and universal fashion might well not disappear quickly, and might very easily be deemed a suitable style for wax dolls to wear, only five or ten years later. Once this is realized, we can look at the doll with fresh eyes, and now "granny's" odd dress can be seen to be very fashionable, and in the bold and careless

Figure 6: This poured wax doll has eyes that close with a wire mechanism, an unusual feature for this type of doll. She's from Winnie Langley's collection.

Bishopsgate, and no where else."

Winnie owns many other unusual wax dolls, among them the unmarked beauty depicted in **figure 6**. This doll has something of the sharp awareness of the one sold by E. Tinker, and it is perhaps due to the sleeping eyes, which are worked with a wire—a mechanism found more often installed in the waxed papier-mâché dolls, a lovely example of which is to be seen in **figure 7**. Also from Winnie's collection, this smiling lady still wears her elaborate commercial dress of the 1850s, and it is in perfect condition, a rare survival that makes the doll doubly desirable—and valuable.

My last, but by no means least, unmarked wax doll is from Dorothy's collection, a lovely child, again wearing those incongruous baby's long clothes. This doll, seen in **figure 8**, has a particularly beautiful complexion; the wax is thick and creamy pink. This, together with the enchantingly puffy eyelids—which make the doll look as if it were going to sneeze—make me wonder if it is not an unmarked Cremer, a very desirable dollmaker working in the mid century. I owned one once, a gentle, slender boy dressed in a cornflower-blue sailor suit, and he is one of the few dolls that I regret parting with. He had very much the look of Dorothy's doll. But I am not sufficiently well acquainted with English waxes to hazard a guess—I can safely leave such identification to English experts like my friend Maree Tarnowska, who handles English waxes every day.

Figure 7: This charming doll above, also from Winnie Langley's collection, wears her original costume of the 1850s. It is in perfect condition.
Figure 8: Although this lovely, unmarked doll at right represents a child, it is dressed in babies' long clothes, a not uncommon thing to find on English Victorian dolls. She's from Dorothy Dixon's collection.

manner of its period. The over sleeves, made to elbow length and longer than the piqué sleeves beneath, are quite remarkably smart, and so is the standing ruff. I have not seen this dress, but I wonder if it is not in fact a Heideloff dress, and the doll is five years earlier than 1800, instead of the declared five years later.

By the time this doll came into Winnie's possession, her dress had become alarmingly fragile, and Winnie chose wisely to lay it away, and to dress the doll in something else. As can be seen from her picture, **figure 5**, she now wears a simple white dress of the period. This doll is marked, not with the name of her maker, alas, but with a most enchanting inscription, and I am surprised Mrs. Early did not share it with us. It is inscribed on the back of its torso in rusty black ink: "To be had of E. Tinker, 54

But I would leave you with this thought: If you are planning to collect English wax dolls, remember that there are many more unmarked wax dolls than there are marked examples, and while it is gratifying to own a marked example, you may have to pay dearly for that signature. The unmarked dolls are just as beautiful, and a skilled expert can hazard a good informed guess as to the maker. There will always be room for doubt, and the true origin may always remain a mystery—but then, I dearly love a mystery, especially when it is a doll.

For my part, I have a weakness for all English wax dolls, marked or unmarked and, given the opportunity, would be delighted to collect dolls of either kind.

Victorian Flower Children

THE AUTHOR DISCOURSES ON SOME OF HIS FAVORITE FLOWERY POSSESSIONS

On my 21st birthday (and oh, what a long time ago that was!) I received a gift from a fellow art student, Marion James, accompanied by a letter that has survived, miraculously, through all the turbulent years between then and now. It detailed Marion's wishes for my future, and in one memorable sentence she wrote, "And since you have so often protested that you cannot live without flowers or music, I wish you these in abundance. All heaven is music, and all its paths are strewn with flowers."

I am delighted to say that Marion's wish came true, and all my life I have been blissfully surrounded by an abundance of music and flowers. So when it comes to dolls, is it surprising that flower dolls hold a very special place in my affections? How avidly I have tried to collect the lovely early chinas and parians—those that wear flowers in their hair—and when I cannot own them, at least I can fill scrapbooks with their photographs. Then there are the later bonnet dolls, the ones called Marguerites, which wear—with enchanting solemnity—flowers and sometimes

insects in place of hats. These too I collect and covet.

There have been many other flower dolls that I have found and rejoiced in as time has gone by, including a number by contemporary artists. And yet it was many years before I discovered that there were wonderful Victorian paper toys and paper dolls that also celebrated the beauty of flowers. None of these ephemeral delights are very common (which, of course, is why I missed out on them for so long), and I take considerable pleasure in presenting here a few of my favorites.

The first of these, a paper doll called Blumenfee or "Flower Fairy," portrays a little girl, in an ordinary blue dress, who can be transformed—as her title promises—into the guardian fairy of six different flowers: the daisy, the violet, the lily, the poppy, the pansy and the forget-me-not. This toy is interesting in that it appears, by the style of the doll's own clothes, to be from the turn of the century, while the engraving of the doll dressed as the poppy fairy, which decorates the box lid, is stylistically from the 1860s or '70s. Examination of the dresses shows that they are die cut, but that the original dresses have obviously been commercially reduced from their once-crinolined silhouettes to a more narrow outline, sometimes causing flowers on the edges of the skirts to be cut in two. There is thus no doubt that the toy was updated for reissue in the late 1890s or early 1900s—and now, of course, I am always hoping to run across the original.

Reviewing the six costumes, I am surprised that there is no rose. All other sets of paper flower-girl toys—be they paper dolls or chromo scraps or greeting cards—all of them honor the queen of the flowers, and I suspect that the early original of the set pictured here would have had eight costumes instead of six, and that one of these would have been the rose.

The paper doll Blumenfee, opposite page, is from the turn of the century, although the design on her box is in the style of the 1860s. The author's copy of The Realm of Flora is shown at left. Painted only recently, the colors are fresh and lovely, unlike the darkened originals.

ical books that were so popular in the 1840s.

This is a most delicious toy to play with—but, of course, the museum's rare and fragile copy was sacrosanct. So, for exhibition purposes, I made a careful photocopy of the toy, which I then hand colored and assembled, to show how it was to be used. And while I was doing this, it occurred to me that from these photocopies I could make my own hand-colored copy to play with.

In the end, I did a little more than this. I traced the outlines of the photocopies onto handmade rag paper, and from these drew my own variation of the original, changing a leaf here and there, or elaborating on some of my own favorite flowers. Otherwise, mine is a fairly faithful copy, and I used the same watercolor pigments that were available in the 1840s.

A surprising bonus came with my set, however—apart from the fact that I can play with it with impunity. One of the sad things about the original set is that either the paper or the painting medium used in the 1840s has darkened with age, so that the original flowers are not quite brown and somber. Mine, on the other hand, drawn on new rag paper and painted so recently, are as fresh as though they were picked this morning.

Although it is not dated, there can be no doubt as to when my third, most glorious paper toy was made, since its dolls are dressed in the height of fashion for the mid 1880s. This is a beautifully boxed toy, and is perhaps the rarest of the three presented here. It is from Germany, and is called, simply, Flora, with the subtitle *Ein Neues Angutiges Ankleide-Spell*. There is a manufacturer's trademark within a crest; it is difficult to read but appears to be: " '*Beluxus Papier-fabrik Berlin,*' *Fabrik-Marke*."

This toy is played with in a manner quite similar to the way that one plays with The Realm of Flora. There are a multitude of cutout, chromo flowers with tiny tabs that must be inserted into slots in the costumes, so that they can be enhanced with the cutout flowers. These figures are also provided with struts, so that they can

My second offering here is an elaborate paper toy called The Realm of Flora. It was published in Germany in the 1840s and is now extremely rare. In fact, for a long time I had only seen poor and fragmentary reproductions of it, until some 15 years ago, when a huge gift of paper toys was made to the Toy Collection of the Museum of the City of New York. This gift is known as the Gold Collection, after its donor, and it contains, amongst many other rarities, a perfect copy of The Realm of Flora.

As can be seen from the illustration on the opposite page, this toy contains several display panels, each depicting an empty vase or urn or basket. Where the flowers should be, there are slits in the display panel, and the toy provides no less than 50 cutout flowers with tabs that can be inserted into the slits to form a bouquet. There is even one panel designed as a wreath, finished off with a large blue bow. The flowers must have been taken from one of the beautifully illustrated botan-

This splendid German paper toy is called Flora. When it was first issued, in the mid 1880s, how exciting it must have been, and how enchanting to play with.

stand. They are most beautifully and intricately printed, with rich and lovely coloring, by chromolithography.

These children are enchantingly dressed. There is a little girl in a party frock, a Swiss peasant girl with pig-tails and another dressed as Marie Antoinette, with a powdered wig. Then there is an older girl with a parasol, another wearing an evening dress with a splendid train and, finally, a bride with her handsome young groom.

Long ago, a very careful child completed all the costumes and then, apparently delighted with her results, neatly pasted paper over the tabs at the back, so that her flowers were fixed permanently in place. In one way this is a pity, since the toy can no longer be played with, but it has the advantage of having preserved the complete figures for over 100 years. And as my fellow collectors will know only too well, toys with loose pieces stand always in danger of losing some of them—and an incomplete toy also loses much of its appeal and much of its value.

But this has not happened to Flora. Everything is in its place within the lovely lace-paper-lined box—the six complete figures, the six little lithographed cards show-

ing how the dolls are to wear their flower decorations (and these are a collector's gem by themselves), the packets of extra flowers and even the sheet of illustrations for the "Flora-Apeil."

Whenever I look at these flowery treasures (and I look at them—indeed, gloat over them—very often), I am most grateful to the people who brought them into my hands. My first thanks go to Gordon Gold, who so generously gave his father's collection, including the Realm of Flora, to my favorite museum. And secondly I must thank two very dear friends, both of whom share with me the joys of collecting paper ephemera. The paper doll Blumenfee was found for me by Grayce Piedmontesi, whom I have known since we were both young enough to walk without canes. And the boxed set Flora came from Maurine Popp, of whose family, so her daughters have told me, I am considered an honorary member.

These are only three examples from my collection of flower-child toys. Perhaps in a future issue we may look at some of the others. But I am sure there are still many other lovely flower dolls and toys, both old and new, that have not yet crossed my path. If any of my readers own or know of such toys and would care to share them with me, I would be both very grateful and very, very delighted!

The Men in Her Life

THE FIRST IN A SERIES ON RARE MASCULINE DOLLS FROM A LEGENDARY COLLECTION

Among the last of the great, legendary doll collections are those of Dorothy Dixon and Winnie Langley. My regular readers will remember that I am lucky enough to live only a mile away from the lovely Colonial house where these two ladies, and their astonishing collections, reside in the greatest felicity.

Readers will also remember that I have been privileged, in the past, to write from time to time about some of the treasures from within these collections. In the course of my explorations therein, I have been struck by the number of rare men and boy dolls that Dorothy has collected. "There is an old idea that men dolls were seldom made," says Dorothy. "But I think that is because the earlier collectors were all focused on little girl and lady dolls. What you aren't looking for," she explains, "you don't see!"

Well, Dorothy certainly sees, and her collection is full of masculine wonders, and choosing which to write about from amongst them makes me feel like a child in a candy store. I was influenced by my great partiality to hatted dolls, a penchant that Dorothy shares, and together we have chosen for publication a mouth-watering selection of treasures: hatted men and boys spanning a period of over a century. And for this article, I proudly present four of the earliest and rarest of these dolls.

They are all of an extremely desirable variety, which maddeningly lacks a proper name. They have molded papier-mâché heads, mounted on stiff-stuffed leather bodies, to which are attached unyielding wooden limbs. As long ago as the 1930s, Yankee collector Eleanor St.

George was writing one of the first doll books, and felt the need of a name for what were amongst her favorite dolls. She boldly coined the quite inaccurate sobriquet: Milliners' Models. This absurdity has stuck to these unlucky dolls for over 60 years—presumably because no pithier or more suitable name has been found—not even by me! The dolls pictured here are all of this variety, and they are all of much the same date, being made in Germany somewhere between 1820 and 1835, and coinciding more or less with what is known in the field of decorative arts as the Biedermeier style. They are all rare and perhaps unique—I certainly have never seen their duplicates.

The doll in **illustration 1** is wearing fancy dress, a highly romanticized version of a Renaissance livery. His jerkin is made of green velvet, perhaps simulating suede leather, and his tan velvet breeches are topped with trunk hose of the same fabric as the jerkin. The thighs and the full-lengths of the sleeves are slashed, showing a cream-colored lining, and the slashes and the bosom of the jerkin are ornamented with silver braiding. The jerkin is topped by a wide collar, purporting to belong to the shirt below, and this, together with the leather hunting bag that is slung from his shoulder, would suggest that this is a gamekeeper's uniform—except that he's wearing a helmet with a visor!

However, a second glance confirms that this is a perfunctory, lip-service helmet, and the visor (or is it a chin guard?) is decorated with stylized wreathes of leaves, lending further credence to my theory that this is the livery of a gamekeeper or perhaps a Ducal huntsman.

The second and third dolls (**illustration 2**) are in costumes contemporary with their manufacture, costumes from the Biedermeier period. These dolls were not made as a pair, but I am enchanted to consider

them as such, since they represent very neatly the fashionable town and country looks of their time.

The rustic gentleman, shown close-up in **illustration 3**, is very young and handsome, with black curls and striking, forget-me-not blue eyes. He wears plum-colored knee-breeches and a fine linen shirt, cut very full with the ballooning sleeves and high standing collar of the period. His braces have double connecting bars in what we think of as the typical Tyrolean style. His beautiful green velour top hat, with its tapering crown and narrow brim, is molded on his head at a pushed back, rakish angle. This is recognizable instantly as a Germanic peasant costume, but it is as well to remember that it was a fashion for the aristocracy to wear the folk costume of their region when residing in their country estates. Also, the lavish and unlikely gold-braid trimmings (whoever heard of gold trimmed breeches, golden braces and a very wide gold belt?)—all this implies to me, at least, fancy dress. It must always be remembered, when puzzling over the dolls of this period, that fancy dress was a popular amusement at that time, and very much in the minds of children.

His companion, seen in **illustration 4**, is a similar doll, but with stronger and more mature features, emphasized by his elegant moustache and side whiskers, and by his melancholy, dark-brown eyes. His town clothes are most dapper, including the new and daring striped "trowsers" that had so recently replaced pantaloons and knee-breeches. His coat (or, as we would call it, his jacket) has fashionably sloping shoulders, with sleeves set in to create slightly puffed shoulders. It has a nipped-in waist, perhaps corseted, which is emphasized by a wide black belt and flaring, full coattails. This coat is braided in black, and is closed with six large black buttons and frogs. His pale-fawn flocked hat is more dandified than that of his rustic friend. The crown is higher and more tapered, and the brim is narrower.

Again, the angle at which it is worn is most stylish and convincing. The last of these four dandies (**illustration 5**) is the most wondrous of all. He represents an officer in a Scottish regiment, and cuts a dashing figure. He is clean shaven and close cropped, although he sports handsome side whiskers. He is tall, with splendid shoulders and a deep chest, and a waistline corseted to a fare-thee-well. (One of the inconveniences of the Battle of Balaklava, we are told, was that it took so long to lace the British officers into their corsets, preparatory to putting on their uniforms!) Above his tartan trews, he wears a waist-length scarlet tunic, smart with gilt buttons, gold braid and epaulettes, and over this he wears, with a swagger, the tartan shawl that is an essential component of Highland dress.

Best of all, molded to his head, is his fantastic bearskin or busby—I do not know the correct name for this towering fur headdress—that folds over to lay a heavy loop of fur down the side of his face. It has a checkered border, an assertive scarlet plume, and an almost invisible chin strap.

I believe it would be hard for you, or for me, to choose a favorite from amongst these four gentlemen. But happily, there is no need. We can all enjoy Lynton Gardiner's beautiful photographs, and sigh over them, while I select the next group, chronologically, of rare hatted men dolls, for the next installment of: "The Men in Her Life."

The Men in Her Life, Part II

A CLOSE-UP LOOK AT SOME MORE WONDERFUL MEN DOLLS

I n our last issue, I was privileged to introduce to you a very special group of dolls, the men dolls that form a part—a small part—of a truly fabulous collection. The collection is that of Dorothy Dixon, who has been gathering her dolls for many years. It has been my great pleasure to choose, from amongst her hosts of men dolls, a select few, the rarest of the rare.

During the 1920s and '30s, when doll collecting was a very young hobby and serious research had not even begun, there had evolved the idea that men and boy dolls were few and far between. We now know that this is a misconception, and since at least the beginning of the 19th century, male dolls have been made wherever

dolls have been made. We also find, to our surprise, that these male dolls were quite often intended as playthings for little boys.

We have only to look at the many illustrations of childhood in books and engravings of the past, to discover little boys playing happily—and rowdily—with dolls dressed as harlequins and Punchinellos, and as brigands and pirates, as well as soldiers of every type. G.I. Joe was by no means the first doll made for the amusement of boys.

It must be remembered, too, that for little girls, the great preponderance of child and toddler dolls is a late-19th-century phenomenon. During the 18th and most of the 19th century, lady dolls were very much more

popular as toys, and they played the roles of companion and confidante to their little owners. But in the evolution and continuation of the dolls' fantasy lives that were the daily play and pleasure of these owners, a male companion was often needed.

A modern and most enchanting example of such fantasy play took place amongst the old dolls that had been collected in the 1940s by the celebrated New England artist, Tasha Tudor, and shared with her young daughter. Ms. Tudor felt that her lovely, crinolined French lady doll had been single for long enough, and she set to work and fashioned for her a handsome suitor, a man doll whom she called Mr. Shakespeare. The French lady looked kindly upon Mr. Shakespeare, their engagement was announced, and

on a summer's day, Tasha's daughter held a wedding party in her garden.

How I would love to have been there! The artist had given full reign to her most romantic fancies, and there was a wonderful wedding dress, a bevy of bridesmaid dolls and bowers of flowers. Afterward, there were presents and a splendid feast, as well as a shower of rice for the happy couple.

Such acting out of dolly's adventures has always been a part of children's play, and it is only logical that boy and men dolls would be needed—and supplied—to take the masculine roles in this everyday amusement. I began this series with some of Dorothy Dixon's earliest dolls, and in this second look, we do not travel much farther forward in time.

Our first doll, shown in **illustration 1**, full-length and close-up, is a dashing soldier from the early years of the 19th century, the time of the Napoleonic Wars. I presume him to be German, since it was one of the great periods of German dollmaking, but this presumption has little to support it. If I could identify his dashing uniform it would be an enormous help, but, alas, in this area I remain in natural ignorance.

I can only say that the doll appears to be carved from wood or fashioned from papier-mâché, and his neck and limbs are ingeniously swiveled. He has been painted with skill and bravura, and even in his stationary position, he seems to swagger—as well he might! He is perhaps a survivor of a set, a squad or platoon of such soldier dolls. With his tough body and

sturdy construction, he would have been a delight to play with.

My second treat today consists of two dolls (**illustration 2**), so very rare and yet so similar that they positively demand to be kept together. They are examples of that very desirable kind of doll made in Germany with stiff leather bodies, wooden limbs and molded papier-mâché heads. I never cease to be astonished by the enormous variety and richness of the dolls of this manufacture, all produced within a span of some 30 or 35 years. There are beautiful ladies and elegant gentlemen, officers in Regimentals, pedlar dolls, and servants of all description, besides a wide variety of ethnic dolls, of which these two are examples.

These very romantic dolls have been conceived as Arabs. Both sport mustaches, and both wear turbans twisted with casual authority (we know at once they have been winding them afresh every day of their lives). One, seen on the right in the photo, is clearly a desert dweller. He wears full trousers and boots, and a voluminous velvet cloak. The other, a gentle-looking soul in a striped shirt, was perhaps intended as a house servant.

My next doll, shown in **illustration 3**, is even more enigmatic, at least to me, since I've never seen another such. This is a gentleman riding to hounds, in his coat of hunting pink. Of course, I am inclined to hope that he is of English origin, since such dashing figures were still part of the English landscape in the days of my youth. There is an indefinable look to this toy that suggests the mid-19th century to me—somewhere near 1860, I should hazard. It is beautifully modeled in papier-mâché, and the hunter is all grace and high spirit.

The gentleman is made separately, and bestrides his horse with great style. He has what is called an "excellent seat." He himself is most elegant, and his pink coat fits with the perfection achieved only by a great tailor—from Saville Row, perhaps? His top hat was the proper headgear for hunting in those days. How proud the first little owner must have been of this beautiful toy!

The last doll in this group is, for me, the most wonderful and tantalizing of all. Shown in **illustration 4**, he is yet another papier-mâché doll, and obviously a very early one. The head is modeled with great vitality and style, and there is a wig set over the modeled locks. This most unusual doll wears a riding costume of an archaic pattern, contrived all of leather. He surely rep-

resents some special character, and pondering on his intense, yearning expression, I wonder if this is perhaps that famous man from La Mancha: the legendary Don Quixote? He has all the wild poetry, and the exalted, removed-from-everyday quality of that strange, impassioned champion of knighthood and chivalry.

Perhaps we shall never know who this marvelous doll represents, but for me at least, this mystery is an irresistible part of the charm of rare and enigmatic dolls, providing us as it does with endless possibilities for dream and conjecture.

There are many other unusual and desirable men dolls on Dorothy's shelves. Next time, we will look at some intriguing chinas and bisques, all from the mid-19th century.

The Men in Her Life, Part III

Once again, with great kindness, Dorothy Dixon has opened the doors to the cupboards and cabinets that house her fantastic doll collection, to give us a glimpse of some more of the wonderful and rare male dolls that she has collected over the years—some of them so rare as to be considered unique.

In previous issues, we have looked at some of Dorothy's earlier gentlemen friends, but today we move forward a few decades. In **illustration 1** we are introduced to three dollhouse dolls. The pair on the right in illustration 1 date, I believe, from the mid-19th century. They are both examples of that desirable kind: German peg wooden dolls with "alien heads" of composition or plaster. The taller of the two is a coachman in a warm gray topcoat. He is obviously an old retainer, much aware

of his responsibilities, and of the trust invested in him. He has, not surprisingly, a serious and introspective demeanor, and this is enhanced by his imposing moustache and his handsome top hat, both molded with his head. The hat is crowned with a splendid plume of feathers, implying that his master is of the aristocracy.

The smaller doll is more humble, a man-in-the-street,

3

Dickens. And how I would have loved and treasured them, if they had come my way when I was a London child!

The third dollhouse doll, a carriage servant (**illustration 2**), is some 50 or 60 years younger than the others. This is a bisque-headed chauffeur from the early days of motoring, when the mere possession of an automobile marked you as a person of wealth and consequence. I once owned a toy automobile of this vintage—it belonged to a lady doll whose prettiness was quite obscured by her huge smothering dust coat, her fearsome goggles and her enormous veiled hat. She sat grandly in the back seat of her open car, driven by a chauffeur doll who wore a bisque peaked cap molded with his head.

He was very nice, but Dorothy's chauffeur is in quite a different class—the carriage servant of a titled lady, surely. He is clad, as you can see, in a splendid scarlet uniform, with much gold frogging, that matches his grand scarlet bisque peaked cap, with its gold badge. He sports an arrogant, upturned mustache and alarming goggles that give him the disquieting air of a predatory insect. But he is very, very rare!

The next group of four dolls are from the 1860s or

4

a sporting man perhaps, wearing the low-crowned, wide-brimmed felt hat (also molded with his head) that we see so often, worn with style and dash, in Victorian genre paintings such as Frith's huge "Derby Day" or his "Ramsgate Sands." (Both pictures were, in their day, huge successes at two of the Royal Academy's annual exhibitions, and both were much admired by Queen Victoria.) This gentleman is very properly dressed for the outdoors on a winter's day, with a high shirt collar and stock, high-necked weskit, jacket and greatcoat, all made at home with carefulness and painstaking attention to detail, which is somehow very touching.

With both these dolls, the signs of age and wear do much to enhance their already considerable charms. As I held the sporting gentleman—he fitted comfortably into the palm of my hand—and as I gazed at his sober-faced friend, the California sunshine faded, and I remembered the mysterious atmosphere of the London streets of my childhood. Those ancient streets retained their layers of memories that were almost palpable on the fog-wreathed autumn nights, when the moon was a ghost, only slightly paler than the gas-lit street lamps. Each of these marvelous men dolls, I felt, would have been at home in one of the rich novels of Charles

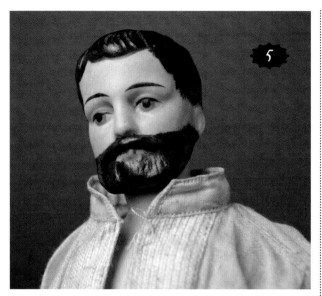

early 1870s, again dollhouse men, but of a superior kind. We have gotten so used to the inch-to-the-foot scale of our later dollhouses—or at least I have—that it comes as a slight shock to realize that some splendid Victorian dollhouses were made on a much larger scale, complete with furniture (including the so desirable mahogany pieces from Waltershausen) and all sorts of accessories, as well as dolls to inhabit and enjoy them. This next handsome quartet are just such dolls.

They all have bisque heads (although similar dolls were put out at the same time with glazed china heads) and are made just like the smaller-scale dollhouse dolls, with bisque extremities and stuffed cotton bodies. All four are unmistakably gentlemen, and the one in evening dress (**illustration 3**), with his dashing scarlet bow tie, is very French-looking, for this is exactly the moustache and goatee made fashionable by Emperor Napoleon III.

The one in **illustration 4**, who wears a very fashionable, narrow-brimmed top hat molded to his head at a very proper angle, is perhaps dressed as a bridegroom, with a spray of lily-of-the-valley in the buttonhole of his frock coat. Unlike his friends—who sport a variety of hirsute ornaments—the possible bridegroom is clean shaven except for his beautifully groomed side-whiskers, known as the time as "Dundrearies" after a lordly character in the popular 1850s play *Our American Cousin* by Tom Taylor.

The gentleman in *déshabillé* (**illustration 5**), whose much pleated shirt-front tells us that he has just removed his own evening coat, is wearing the full beard that always makes me think of the British navy, whose gallant

lads were required to be either clean shaven or to wear their full beards; all half measures were frowned upon. A charming touch to this most charming doll is that his crisply cropped hair has been painted with a warmer and paler brown than his beautiful beard. Beards are not common today, but during the 1970s they saw a great revival, and it was amusing to see again young men with, say, dark-brown hair, but startlingly ruddy beards!

The last of this four, shown in **illustration 6**, is the finest, and perhaps the rarest. Here is a splendid bisque head, beautifully modeled, with well-defined lower eyelids and the most engaging, elusive half smile. This doll has a curly head of hair that is painted a lively chestnut color, and his equally curly beard follows his jawline, but leaves his upper lip and chin smooth. I wore the same

beard myself during the 1950s, but mine, alas, could never have equaled this doll's for curly effulgence. (A note on popular slang: Were his entire chin clean shaven, the resultant side-whiskers would be of the shape known as the time as mutton-chop whiskers, a nickname almost obsolete today, for how often do you see a mutton chop? I never do.)

Again, this is only a sample of the marvelous, rarely seen men dolls offered so generously for our delight by my dear friend, Dorothy Dixon. There are many more to choose from. When I sit in Dorothy's parlor, armfuls of dolls laid out for me to see, I feel like a little boy again, in a candy store! And that in itself is a rare, rare pleasure.

The Men in Her Life, Part IV

A FINAL LOOK AT SOME RARE FELLOWS

Today, for the fourth and concluding time, Dorothy Dixon opens her legendary doll cabinets for us, this time to show us some rare fellows from the time of the great German character dolls. As before, the variety was bewildering, but in the end we chose eight dolls, all, as always, as rare as hen's teeth!

Our first choice is the earliest in time, I think, for the handsome chap shown in **illustration 1** seems related to some of the soldiers that we have looked at

in previous articles, and could be of much the same date, the 1870s. His bisque face and painted eyes are full of liveliness and character. He wears a gray helmet with a chin strap and a jaunty plume, and it sits so seriously on his head that one is sure it represents an officer's helmet of a particular regiment. His moustache, goatee and even his eyebrows are beautifully groomed, and one remembers with a smile the vanity of young officers, especially, it would seem, in Austria, in those glamorous days.

Our second man, shown in **illustration 2**, is hard to date, although his muttonchop whiskers imply the late 1860s to early 1870s. This is a most lively and witty lit-

3

1890s, or perhaps around the turn of the 20th century. He has a most beautiful head, marvelously modeled, and with painted intaglio eyes. His gray mohair wig is now disheveled, but it once represented the crisp, military wig commonly worn by officers in the 18th century. The future president is portrayed with dignity and sadness. It comes as a surprise to find this realistic head mounted on a very stylized doll's body, and then to discover that the doll sits astride an unmistakably toy horse. This discrepancy is not unpleasing, and it gives vitality—even urgency—to this unusual toy. And when we examine it closely there is another surprise, and an unlike one—for this is a candy box!

Our fourth, fifth and sixth dolls, who have been photographed, very appropriately, as a group in **illustration 4** seem to be political caricatures. They are similar in style and character, and are somewhat later than the cigar smoker, from a period of unrest and conquest and victory. There are many such dolls dating from about this time—Earl Horatio Herbert Kitchener and Earl Frederick Sleigh Roberts dolls, for instance, were made most successfully for patriotic little English boys.

The military man here is the tallest and most striking of the three—indeed, he dwarfs the other two gentlemen. His bisque head with its red wig and brilliant blue glass eyes is extremely characterful. His delicate mouth is offset by his patrician nose and the wrinkles of concern on his forehead. This head is marked "SL." He has metal hands and legs, but bisque boots with definitely molded buttons, implying gaiters.

The man in the gray suit has a startled look, but this is perhaps just the way that the light has caught his pale-blue glass eyes. He has a simple five-piece composition body, and his curly mohair wig was chosen with great care, since it matches exactly his painted beard.

The man in the black coat is most interesting, since he wears a partial wig, just as a gentleman might wear a

tle fellow; his cheap, poorly made body, with its pot belly and crude wooden hands and feet, belies the wonderful bisque head, with its painted eyes and mouth modeled open to hold his cigar. On the other hand, his beautiful, shining silk hat is most carefully made, leading one to wonder if this were perhaps an advertising doll for a hatmaker, like the famous lady disguised as a parlor maid, who holds a tray with a cup of steaming chocolate.

But a closer look dispels such thoughts, for we are too busy marveling and conjecturing. For this doll has a bisque body, into which the arms and legs are wired, and his potbelly is a rubber ball, from which a tube runs up, inside his head to his mouth. The precise way in which this mechanism worked we shall perhaps never know, but his secret is clearly revealed—this was a smoking doll. But why? Did he advertise a brand of cigars, perhaps? Or is this one of the political caricatures that was beginning to be popular?

Our third doll, seen in **illustration 3**, is even earlier, at least in its depiction, for it is a portrait of the young George Washington, although it was made in the

toupee. His painted gray hair is molded from a center part, and again is molded to define his hairline at the back. He, like his companions, has beautiful handmade eyes. He is marked "17D."

This most remarkable—and covetable—group present us with three mysteries, for surely all of these dolls were intended as portraits of men in the public eye at the time. But who were they?

I have saved my two favorites till last, and I cannot decide which of the two I would snatch up to save from a blazing building. The portrait head (**illustration 5**) is from the Edwardian period, roughly from 1900-1910. This is the heyday of the wonderful German character dolls, many of whom were obviously made by sculptors of the first rank; so it is with this handsome gentleman here. Caught at the moment when he turned his head, his face is alight with interest and pleasure. It is a speaking likeness, I am sure, and this head, without the slightest alteration, could be blown up to life-size, cast in bronze, and could take its place proudly, with any other portraiture of the period.

There is an amusing coincidence here, for the doll has been made with a shoulder head and sew holes, like hundreds of others. But it so happens that, at the time, there was a fashion for young gentlemen—and some darling ladies, too—to be photographed with bare shoulders. There exists just such a portrait of the beautiful and tragic young English poet Rupert Brooke (1887-1915), and the photographer must have made a fortune, so many copies of it, in silver frames, graced the boudoirs of emotional young ladies!

My last doll (**illustration 6**) is a rare and wonderful Saint Nicholas. To date him is difficult, since there are no others like him, but he is made of a very fine bisque, beautifully modeled and painted, and his beard and elaborate turban headdress are modeled in the bisque, like the so-desirable fancy bisque ladies of the 1870s and 1880s. I suspect that this is where he can be placed, and earlier rather than later.

In any case, he is for me the most marvelous of all Dorothy's rare gentlemen. If I betray a little subjective envy here, it is because Saint Nicholas has always been my favorite saint, and I am sad when he degenerates into the commercialized and trite Santa Claus. But this is my own Saint Nicholas, strong and pure and gentle. You know he would never miss your stocking, however inaccessibly deep in the country you lived.

And so I must conclude my blissful exploring through Dorothy's enchanting cabinets. She is so patient, and so pleased to share her treasures, but I feel I have imposed on her for long enough, just for the present. Next time, who knows? Dorothy Dixon and her friend Winnie Langley have many other cupboards and cabinets, the thought of which sets me plotting and planning afresh. Meanwhile, I am pleased to say that *Dolls* magazine, as well as Dorothy and I, have all been given ample proof of the pleasure and delight that these glimpses of Dorothy's gentlemen friends have brought to our readers. And this makes me very humble, and very, very proud.

PART III

1993-1995

In his later articles, the author takes pleasure in the "Aladdin's treasury of objects" he loves, from delicious early English woodens to desirable documented chinas and shabby, untouched dolls' houses.

A Trunk Full of Treasures

TWO LITTLE CHINA HEADS AND THEIR WARDROBES

It is quite a small doll's trunk, iron-bound and covered with leather, very plain and businesslike. Upon opening it, we find it to be packed to the brim with small, oblong boxes, ten of them; they are beautiful shiny boxes made of what used to be called pasteboard. By their style, they can be dated to the mid-1860s. These small boxes have labels printed in a rich royal blue. "GEORGE A. CLARK" they read, and then "Sole Agent, Clark's 'OUR NEW THREAD' for hand and machine sewing. 50,60,70,80, Warranted 6 cord." Today, such pretty boxes are very collectible, and so they were, it appears, at the time when they were made. By a lucky chance, they fit very neatly into this serious, sober-sided trunk.

Fascinated, we open the blue, decorated cover to the dome of the trunk's lid, to find two adorable little dolls—a lady and a gentleman—gazing out at us from amongst their wrappings. They have the beautiful glazed china heads and limbs so typical of the 1860s. They are of precisely the same manufacture. Looking at them, one is sure that they were bought together, and chosen carefully, too, for he is slightly taller at 6½ inches high. The lady is only 4½ inches and comes just to his shoulder. They are a well-matched, romantic-looking pair.

One of the boxes contains the gentleman's few possessions, and another is full of bed linens, sheets and pillowcases, one of which has the name "May" printed on it. The rest of the boxes—there seem to be dozens of them, but there are just eight in number—contain the lady's wardrobe. Dress after lovely dress

These two little dolls (the groom is 6½ inches high) from the "treasure trunk" have the beautiful glazed china heads so typical in the 1860s.

Among the trunk's treasures are a box of bed linens, sheets and pillowcases; a half-mourning dress and black lace bertha; and green, pink and blue silk afternoon dresses.

appears as we open the boxes in a trance of pleasure; everything dates from the later years of the 1860s. There are sparkling cotton prints for morning wear, afternoon dresses of silk in apple green and rose pink and a deliciously deep, delphinium blue. Indeed, spread before us on the table, this wardrobe looks like a bunch of flowers, and freshly picked, too, so immaculately have they been preserved in their boxes. There are enchanting accessories, sashes and garters, caps and bonnets, an "ermine" muff, underclothes, and a beautifully stitched and tucked nightdress. And there is a hat to match each pretty costume, too.

There is a dark-gray silk dress with black lace trimming, together with a black lace bertha, and this is perhaps the ubiquitous half-mourning costume, in which the ladies of that period seemed to spend so many of their days. Best of all is the wedding dress, with its wide, wide crinoline, a tour de force of creamy satin and frothing lace.

The gentleman doll fares poorly in comparison, but his own formal black suit is handsomely made, as befits a bridegroom. He does own a separate striped and starred calico shirt, and very interesting it is. Used together, the patterns combine to create a most unusual print. This shirt is exquisitely cut and sewn—and it must be remembered, looking at our illustrations, that these garments are very tiny.

To accompany this shirt is a round box labeled

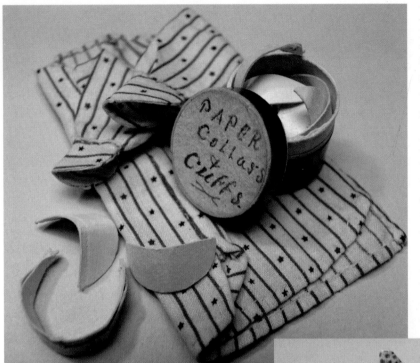

Although the groom's wardrobe is not as extensive as his bride's, he does have the striped and spotted shirt shown at top and a box of paper collars and cuffs. The cotton print, right, is one of the bride's morning dresses.

work of a little girl, supervised by Nanny or the governess, or even doting Mama, and they were her first lessons in stitchery. But this particular trousseau is so competently conceived and executed that one is sure it is the work of a skilled grownup.

Was it an older sister, perhaps? I have seen several nice examples of toys made by older children for the amusement of younger siblings. Or was it that doting Mama, who sat and sewed these tiny garments during lazy summer afternoons in the garden, or long winter afternoons by the fireside while the snow drifted by the window? What stories were invented about this pretty couple, preserved for us on their wedding day in the late 1860s?

"Paper Collars & Cuffs," and sure enough, those are its contents, spotlessly clean and virginal. This is most interesting to me because my own memory of paper collars is of my father, and it dramatizes the extreme poverty of his childhood in the 1880s. He described with feeling the ignominy of having to wear collars of paper to school when his classmates were provided with linen ones. But earlier, in the late 1860s, it seems, such paper accessories were considered both novel and smart.

Nothing is known of the history of this treasure, not even its place of origin, although one assumes from the box labels that it is American. But one is free to speculate, and the mind races over the possibilities, while the eye admires. Clearly, this was a special toy for a little girl from the middle class, not rich, but comfortably circumstanced. It was valued and treated with great respect, for there is no sign of wear and tear. Everything is as crisp and clean as if made yesterday.

And made, too, with exquisite care and precision, every seam perfect, every hem minutely stitched. Often, it seems to me, such wardrobes for small dolls were the

It is the time when Lewis Carroll was weaving his magic tales for his adored Alice, when Edward Lear was stringing together his enchanting nonsense, and when Louisa M. Alcott was fondly describing her little women. It was a time that produced such delights as this little trunkful of marvelous treasures, with its offering of endless, fascinating speculations.

The happy owner of this little wonder is my dear friend, Dorothy Dixon, and *Dolls* joins me in thanking her for her kindness in sharing it with us.

Pedlars & Charity Bazaars

THE IRRESISTIBLE FASCINATION OF TINY THINGS FOR SALE

I own, and love, three sets of pedlar dolls, those fascinating old toys that were not intended as playthings for children but rather as treasures to be kept under glass, so as to display the intricate skills needed to fashion all the tiny items "offered for sale." These toys came into my life long ago, in the 1940s. They were snatched away and lost for over 30 years, to come back only lately into my possession, safe and unharmed.

Their remarkable and romantic story was set out in the May/June 1987 issue of this magazine; I have sought out other pedlars to present to you today. The five beauties chosen are all from the collection of Dorothy Dixon, so it is not surprising that they are, every one of them, extremely unusual, the rarest of the rare.

The earliest pedlar here is also, perhaps, the rarest. This lovely single doll (**illustration 1**), only five inches high, must surely date from the beginning of the 19th century. She has a rare shoulder head of papier-mâché, and a homemade body with stitched leather hands. Her fragile paper costume has the high waist of the period, and her striped violet dress, faded now to lilac, is protected by an olive-green apron striped with a richer green. This dress has the "new" long sleeves described in Jane Austen's *Pride and Prejudice*, published in 1813, and a fashionable low neckline, filled in with a paper-lace fichu. Her headdress is a turban, also very fashionable, of striped paper in two shades of apricot. Her tray is unusual, shaped as it is to fit comfortably at the waist. Most of her wares have disappeared, but what remain are fresh strawberries, temptingly arranged on their own green leaves, suggesting that she was a fruit seller. She wears surprisingly busi-

This five-inch-high pedlar, with a shoulder head of papier-mâché, is believed to date from the beginning of the 19th century.

2

nesslike black shoes and scarlet stockings. This, together with her elegant paper costume, suggests to me that she is French, and perhaps made for a bazaar by one of the aristocratic French émigrés to be found in England in the early 1800s.

Next, we have a pair of pedlars from the 1830s (**illustration 2**), and they are made in the manner of the well known commercially manufactured pedlars labeled "White of Portsmouth." But these are home-made examples. Their modeled kid-leather faces are

These two homemade pedlars are from the 1830s. Their paint-ed faces are modeled of kid leather and they carry mostly homemade wares.

coarser than those of the White dolls, and they have painted complexions, which gave them much more vivid features.

Their rustic clothing is carefully fashioned, and the homely wares in their baskets are a joy to contemplate. A few nice objects are from a dollhouse: the

A rare waxed wooden, this circa-1850s pedlar, above and at right, is in perfect condition. Her wig is set in a split and her eyes open and close.

I have a great weakness for the collections of toys that were assembled under glass during the early 19th century and displayed in the parlor. They are usually English, and I suspect that these pretty objects were often memorials to deceased infants. But there was also a tradition for such glass cases amongst the gentry. These were some of the trophies brought home from their finishing schools by the young ladies of the house

hairbrush, the hallmarked silver scissors, the playing cards and the corkscrew. But everything else seems to be homemade: the exercise books, the mops and dusters, the net cap, the cards of jewelry and the sewing notions. Best of all, to my eyes, are the balls of soap, neatly wrapped and minutely labeled.

Our next pedlar (**illustration 3**) is a little later, from the 1850s. This doll is a lovely and rare waxed wooden, in perfect condition. Her wig is set in a split, and her eyes are wired to open and close. Her dress is checkered silk, and she wears a most practical pocketed apron and a cap decorated with a bow of ribbon. She has the ubiquitous red cape that was worn about the countryside at that time, not only by pedlars but by most women, even ladies.

Her tray and apron pockets contain a variety of delicious objects, including a tiny posy of silk violets, miniscule handmade baskets, card cases and needle books, lace-edged kerchiefs, ribbons and laces, and silver thimbles. Best of all is a collection of tiny valentines, many sealed with red wax, and one of them cut out in the form of a tiny white dove.

Dating from the second quarter of the
19th century, this scene of peg woodens
depicts a stall at a charity bazaar.

charming and delicate, with most of
them contrived from the perforated
cardboard sold at that time as a
ground for cross-stitch needlework.
There are other baskets on the table,
as well as pincushions, purses, boxes
and lamp mats. Many of these articles are beautifully decorated with
beadwork. There are four tiny wood-
en dolls for sale, one of which is a pen
wiper. Crocheted mats adorn the
walls, adding to the pervading atmosphere of richness and gaiety. This case
can never have been opened, for everything in it is
as fresh and sparkling as when it was new.

The last of Dorothy's delights for today is also a

to demonstrate their accomplishments. These trophies included embroidered samplers and memorial
pictures, painted screens and decorated workboxes,
landscapes and vases of flowers
made in shellwork.

Just such a glass case is our next
example here, and it represents a
stall at a charity bazaar (**illustration 4**). It dates from the second
quarter of the 19th century, and
the dolls are the jointed peg woodens from Bavaria. Two soberly
dressed wooden ladies sit behind
the stall and wait on the four customers—two ladies, a boy and
girl—all dressed in their best to
attend this charity affair.

The stall has a pink silk
cover, draped in white
net, and this conceit is
repeated in the ruched
curtains at the top of the
case, providing a rich and elegant
setting for the objects offered for
sale. Such bazaars were run by
church groups, or ladies clubs, and
the members vied with each other
to produce pretty pieces of fancy
work.

A rod runs from one side of the
stall to the other, and it carries no
less than 16 baskets, all of them

Another stall at a charity bazaar, tended by glazed china dolls, this scene dates a bit later, and is more serious, than the one in the case.

stall for a charity bazaar (**illustration 5**), and it, too, I feel sure, was made to be sold at just such a bazaar. This toy is later than the others shown here; it dates from the mid-1860s. It is a very serious object, especially when contrasted with the frivolous toy we have just discussed. The sales table has been carefully made, with turned mahogany legs; the iron rail protecting three sides is held up by turned supports of mahogany. There is a pale-blue silk cover edged with lace and upon it repose some very ambitious items of fancywork indeed.

Besides the objects that one might expect—the beaded misers purses and the pincushions—there are such delights as rolls of sheet music and embroidered cases to contain them, a harlequin purse made in Berlin-work, a battledore and shuttlecock, and charmingly painted and embroidered hand screens. On the floor below the stall are to be found three beautiful footstools worked in petit point. There are a few commercial objects intended for dollhouses—the pewter bell; the copper dishes; and that rare object, the ivory *bilboquet* (a cup and ball game), a child's toy that is held in the hand of one of the presiding ladies.

And very special ladies these are, glazed china dolls with articulate wooden bodies, a most desirable variety. They are soberly but most sumptuously dressed, and their sweet but serious faces emphasize the dedication and care with which this enchanting toy was made.

The reader is permitted a sigh—or perhaps five sighs—of envy. The writer can only be grateful that he lives so close to these enchanting treasures.

A Very Sweet French Lady

THE BEAUTIFUL BRIDE HIDES A DELIGHTFUL SURPRISE

I love surprises and so, it seems, did the luxury-loving young ladies of the 1870s and '80s. In previous articles I have discussed dolls that had been created as novelties for those lucky young women. We have seen dolls turned into pincushions and pen wipers, into vanity bags and sewing companions. I have found dolls that tell fortunes or the day of the month, and all sorts of other delightful contrivances.

The function of most of these pretty things is obvious at first glance but sometimes their purpose is deliberately hidden, a surprise. A pincushion may be hidden under a billowing crinoline; an innocent basket carried on a china arm may contain a thimble and scissors, needles and thread wax. Those are the ones that I love the most, for, as I have said, I dearly love a surprise.

The lady doll pictured here is innocent looking enough and desirable enough to make any collector's mouth water. Her classic bisque swivel head, marked "R.C. Déposé," is swooningly lovely, and it is on a

Around the neck of this swooningly lovely swivel head is "something blue."

molded shoulder plate that is unusually deep. The lady's bisque hands are on bisque arms that extend to the shoulder. Both her clothes and wig are unmistakably original. Brides are always romantic, and this dress of ivory faille silk is perfectly delicious, as its first owner might have said in the fashionable slang of the time. It dates from the early 1880s.

The bodice is very simple, with its princess lines, the only ornaments being a satin bow at the low,

square neck and the complicated pleating of satin bands at the cuffs. The skirt is narrow, pulled back into a full train behind. It is shirred to the knee, where it breaks into a froth of ruching and pleating. To add to this richness, there is an inset panel down the front, implying an open dress and a petticoat.

This faux extravagance is of deeply ruched satin. It is ornamented with a spray of cambric orange blossoms, and these time-honored wedding flowers also appear at the cuffs, in a spray across the train, and in the bouquet. There is a perfunctory tiara of blossoms, which must be the remnant of a more ornate headdress, attached to a most lovely veil of handmade lace.

Traditionally, for the English at least, a bride should always wear: "Something old, something new, something borrowed and something blue." Here the lovely veil is certainly older than the doll, and she may well have borrowed some of her orange blossoms from amongst the souvenirs of a real bride. Her necklace is blue, made of the beautiful turquoise glass beads that we have come to associate with the French ladies of this period, and it is surely original to her. This is an unusual touch. Indeed, I cannot remember ever to have seen a bride, of any period, sporting a blue necklace. But it is an original, fresh and delightful idea, one of which any prospective bride amongst my readers might perhaps take notice!

All this is enchanting and covetable, and one sighs with the special pleasure that comes from viewing a fine original French lady doll. However, when we pick her up and examine her more closely, we find that she is fastened to a circular brocade-covered stand and upon lifting her skirts (with great care and respect), we discover that she wears heeled satin slippers with silk bows

Hidden beneath this bride's gown, naughtily perched atop her silken legs, is her surprise: a candy box

"Did I show you my beautiful new bride doll; isn't she lovely? And would you care for a chocolate?"

maids, their uncomfortable lace-up morning costumes, replacing them with elaborate dressing gowns, known in France as *robes de chambre*, in which they could receive afternoon callers. This was the time of day when young ladies could visit their friends for tête-à-têtes, for cozy confidences over cups of tea, or the French *tisane*.

"Did I show you my beautiful new bride doll; isn't she lovely? And would you care for a chocolate?" The surprise and delight of the visitor is easy to imagine. The novelty would soon have worn off, of course, but the delight would remain. The doll would in time become a little legend and would be passed down from generation to generation, an unusual family treasure.

And she is still treasured. This candy box bride doll, so unusual and lovely, belongs to my dear friend Dorothy Dixon, and was one of the treasures that she offered to *Dolls* when Lynton Gardiner flew out from New York last August and Dorothy, again, with great patience and sweetness, opened her legendary cupboards for us. Lynton spent two glorious days behind his camera in Dorothy's house so my readers may turn the page secure in the knowledge that Dorothy, Lynton and I have several other delightful treats in store for you in future issues.

and, most adorable and provocative, ribbed silk stockings.

And now we discover the bride's hidden surprise, for her bisque legs end at the knee in an oval box of shining white pasteboard. This is the kind of box very familiar to those of us who collect the old Dresden Christmas ornaments, which often conceal a tiny candy box made of this identical pasteboard. To our astonishment—or at least, to my own—the upper part of the doll, when lifted, glides smoothly upward and away, taking with it the elaborate skirt, the train and the veil. There, perched surrealistically on top of those naughty silken legs, is a candy box.

We exclaim with delight, and it is easy to imagine the original recipient's own delight before us. This was the heyday of boudoirs, of those afternoon retreats where fashionable ladies could retire after luncheon in private to remove, with the help of their

Let's Play at Weddings

THESE SMALL ENGLISH DOLLS HELPED A VICTORIAN GIRL TO ACT OUT HER MATRIMONIAL DREAMS

I suppose playing at weddings may well be one of the most popular games of little girls, everywhere and always. It certainly must have been for 19th- and 20th-century English and American girls, to judge by the evidence of the wedding dolls left behind. As one would expect, there are wedding dolls to be found in other countries, too. There are wonderful folk bride dolls from India, all glittering with gauze and gilt papers. There are African brides encrusted with beads, to say nothing of Scandinavian and Russian and Polish and Hungarian brides, all splendidly dressed in their regional finery. I love them all, sentimental old fool that I am. But my special affection is reserved for the wedding dolls from my own country (England), and from the 19th century.

Last August, Lynton Gardiner flew out to visit us here in California, and Dorothy Dixon opened her magical doll cupboards for us, looking for treasures to be photographed. "How would you like a wedding?" she

This wonderfully absurd little wedding group, in which the adults are all made with the same blond bisque head, dates from the late 19th century. The ambitious wedding party features a best man, groom, bride, clergyman, three bridesmaids, flower girl and ring bearer.

Although the head with its plump cheeks and its lovely inset cornflower-blue glass eyes is pretty for the bride, it sits oddly upon the groom.

asked, as she produced the group of dolls depicted here, little dolls, about six inches high. And you can imagine our delight, Lynton's and mine, for this is the most charmingly absurd little wedding! But we must be careful not to laugh, for it was surely put together very seriously, and great pains were taken with every detail.

The ambitious wedding party dates from the late 19th century. We have a bride and groom, a best man, three bridesmaids, a flower girl and a ring bearer. And, conveniently, a clergyman. But why ever was the very feminine bisque head—chosen surely as very suitable

for a bride—used again, blithely, not only for the bridesmaids, but also for the manly groom, his best friend, and the benighted clergyman? It is a very common but pretty head, with its demure plump-cheeked face and its lovely inset cornflower-blue glass eyes that lend it a somewhat startled expression. But it has been used indiscriminately for all the adult dolls here, and it sits very oddly upon the gentlemen.

Seven blond heads must have looked a trifle monotonous, so the gentlemen's hair was given a coat of black paint, now mostly worn away, which stiffened their characters a little. But one wonders, with great pleasure, how this duplication came about—for there were many different dolls' heads available at that time. A conversation long ago, with my dear friend Vivien

So they stand before us, this wedding party, wide-eyed while the troth is plighted.

Greene, may provide an answer. "You must remember," she said, "that children's toys were mostly a very trivial matter then...and also, England was largely rural. The local general store may have had a poor selection, but what was there was bought, and the child was not critical." This may well have been the case here. Mummy or Aunty or bigger sister bought seven of these beauties with her saved-up pennies because they were available.

However it came about, the results, you will agree, are felicitous, and we would have them no other way. The dolls have been dressed with care but with no very great skill, attention being focused, very properly, upon the bride with her three flounces of real lace, her ruched bodice, crystal necklace, and her bouquet of enormous flowers, endearingly out of scale. The bridegroom and his friend are sketchily clad in surprising light-blue suits. Was this the local fashion at a country wedding or was this, more than likely, the only cloth available to the seamstress? The clergyman's vesture is serious but unidentifiable—is this a cope and stole, perhaps, white for a wedding? The bridesmaids' dresses are elaborately flounced and puffed, and one suspects them to have been cut down from part of an outdated full-sized costume. The children have been dressed with greater skill—perhaps by a different hand—and the little girl is fashionable and charm-

ing. Different and suitable heads, with brown glass eyes, were chosen here.

So they stand before us, this wedding party, wide-eyed while the troth is plighted. And with politely concealed amusement we notice that the same head can register different emotions. The bride is confident; the bridegroom apprehensive; the best man trustworthy and ready for any contingency; the clergyman grave and responsible; the bridesmaids—all three of them—are anticipating!

How this enchanting group came about we may never know, but the pleasure that they give is as rare as it is delightful! And I am reminded, as I gaze at this assembled wedding party, of the elopement planned by the lovers in Gilbert and Sullivan's *H.M.S. Pinafore*:

A clergyman shall make us one
(At half-past ten) and then
We can return, for none
Shall part us then…

So sing those Victorian lovers, and who knows? Maybe this little wedding was inspired by one of those operettas, so universally known and loved, which are all informed with a similar very English sense of the absurd!

The dolls have been dressed so that attention is focused on the bride with her three flounces of real lace, ruched bodice, and bouquet of out-of-scale flowers. The bridegroom and his friend are sketchily clad in surprising light-blue suits and the clergyman's vesture is serious but unidentifiable. The child has been dressed with greater skill than the others, perhaps by a different hand.

The Cheating Cardplayer

These days, I am no longer an active collector. Like the legendary ladies of Boston, who had their hats and their antiques, I have my dolls and my dollhouses. But in the days when I did collect, I was as avid and passionate in the pursuit of my prizes as anyone. In particular, I loved to own dolls that had once belonged to the famous collectors of the past. Regular readers may recall that I wrote of this particular passion in a past issue ("Collectors Collected," May 1991). And of all those legendary collectors, the one who haunts me the most is the enigmatic Henri d'Allemagne.

D'Allemagne was one of the very first serious collectors of dolls and toys and certainly one of the first to write about them. He lived in Paris at the end of the last century, during the last great era of European dollmaking, but he was an antiquarian, and so, of course, the dolls in which he took so obsessive an interest were of a much, much earlier date. He was an incurable romantic, and his writings are fascinating.

He lived well into this century; his splendid, costly books were published during its first decade, and his collections remained shut up in his house in Paris right through World War II. My old friends the late Ruth and Bob Mathes, visited Paris in the early 1950s, and they were invited to the D'Allemagne house by a descendant and were shown the sealed, dusty rooms where his dolls and toys slept, peaceful and undisturbed.

That was a long time ago, and much has happened since. During the 1980s, when I was still collecting, dolls from the D'Allemagne hoard began to appear on the American market. I was lucky enough, through the good offices of my friend Richard Wright, to acquire several pieces. They are all remarkable and all equally treasured, but perhaps my favorite piece is the one I call The Cheating Cardplayer.

It is from the late 17th century and is covered with a five-sided wooden-framed glass case. This fits snugly into

The author's Cheating Cardplayer is a piece once owned by the legendary collector Henri d'Allemagne. Dating from the late 17th century, it features four German wax dollhouse dolls in a glass case. It is the lady on the right, dressed in ivory silk and a jacket of embroidered silk net, who is the cheat, hiding a card in a fold of her skirt. Note the blue and yellow snake slithering, unnoticed by the group, at her feet.

a wooden base with deep molding and bun feet. There is a fretted parapet, and there were once finials, of which a solitary one remains. All the goldleaf woodwork is crumbling now so that the gesso is beginning to show. The glass panes are of the old hand-blown "crown glass," lively and glittering with its natural imperfections.

On the floor of this case is a red silk brocade carpet, now fragile and much faded, and set upon it are a round table and four chairs. This flimsy wooden furniture, innocent of paint or varnish, is recognizable from the 17th-century dollhouses; there is a similar suite in the parlor of Anne Sharp's House in England, for instance. The card-players are recognizable, too. They are the German wax dollhouse dolls that were made in great quantities, as evidenced by those that survive, during the late 17th and 18th centuries. They have wax heads and limbs, with curious beady black eyes, and they have perfunctory bodies of wire and wrapped straw. It is amazing that so many have survived. The ones here were particularly lucky, for they were set up with their card game during the 1690s, and they have remained safely inside their very solid glass case ever since. To this day, they are undisturbed, and incredibly enough, they still sit in the postures in which they were arranged so very long ago.

There are three ladies and a gentleman playing cards, and it is one of the ladies, I'm afraid, who's cheating, hiding a card in a fold of her skirt. They are most fashionably

Two of the women wear unusual fontanges, which have been seen in period paintings. They are velvet caps, rather than lace, that rear up away from the head.

dressed, these ladies, but the gentleman is at home, and he has thrown off his great wig with its corkscrew curls, together with his heavy gold-laced coat and waistcoat. He wears instead the comfortable but very fashionable *déshabillé* of the time, a *banyon*, which we today would call a dressing gown. Its costly fabric is fine Persian silk; its printed pattern is in cream on an indigo ground. His cravat is fine lace, and he wears a blue velvet cap with a black faux-fur brim. By contrast,

the ladies are formally dressed for the evening with elaborate gowns and the complicated fontange head-dresses so typical of this period.

One lady, the cheat, wears a fine plain ivory silk gown with a knee-length jacket of embroidered silk net. Her apron is similar and her high fontange is a conventional one, lavishly trimmed with lace. The other ladies wear brocades with full pleated brocade aprons. Both their costumes are trimmed with silver bullion fringe.

Their fontanges are similar to each other but very different from that of the first lady. They have no froth of lace, but rather severe velvet caps set on the back of their heads with curving pieces that cover their ears. From the forehead a stiff padded fold of the velvet rears up into the air. There are ribbon trimmings, but no hair is to be seen; nothing softens the outrageous smartness of these two headdresses. My friend David Walker is an internationally known stage designer and an expert on costume, and he became very excited when he saw these two strange headdresses. "I've seen them before in portraits of the period," he says, "But I've never found a real one, not in all the museum collections that I've researched. These dolls may be wearing the only examples left extant!"

This is a marvel indeed, and it is a marvel, too, that these clothes are in such perfect condition, for there is very little stitchery. The clothes are held together largely by tiny pins, the handmade straight pins of the 16th century with their minute heads looking like seed pearls. This is enormously interesting to me, for it is a reminder that, in those far-off days, a lady's toilette was invented on the spot with the help of her imaginative and talented lady's maid. Complete, finished dresses as we know them didn't exist. Petticoats, open robes, panniers, stomachers, lace ruffles and fichus, all these elements would be assembled on the whim of the moment, tacked, perhaps, but most likely *pinned* together in a combination planned to last for only one evening. The pins were expensive and, of course, easily lost, so that a lady needed a good supply of *pin money* to insure her elegant appearance—beside a battery of pincushions!

A chandelier hangs above the cardplayers, a charming one of crystal and white and turquoise-blue glass. It is very pretty, but it is a commercial dollhouse chandelier from Lauscha and was made perhaps as late as 1870. It was added, no doubt, to replace the original, which I suspect would have been a brass one. What happened to it, I wonder?

There is one other significant object, and this is original to the piece, I'm sure. A small blue and yellow snake is slithering, unnoticed, from under the skirts of the cheating lady. It is of Nevers glass and is of the same date as the rest of the scene. Its meaning remains obscure and tantalizing.

The sole gentleman of this group seems to be at home. He's apparently taken off his wig, coat and waistcoat and sits playing in his dressing gown.

There is one last delight. Hidden under the *banyon* skirt, I discovered a little card. On one side is printed in French: "Exhibition of dolls, from the 4th to the 20th of May, 1935, Strasbourg." On the back, handwritten, is the magic name: "M. Henri D'Allemagne, case 4."

D'Allemagne must have been an elderly man by 1935 and proud and protective of his treasures, gathered together so lovingly when almost no one else cared. Well, Monsieur, I care, and you may rest assured that such treasures of yours that have come into my possession, including this delightful card-playing party, will be loved and protected at least for my time.

In Concert with Jenny Lind

A ROMANTIC STORY THAT TOOK PLACE IN NEW YORK
AND HAS SPANNED A CENTURY AND A HALF

In each generation, amongst all its famous and desirable women, there are always those who stand out above the others, who seem to typify the dreams and desires of the women of their day. In our own time, for instance, it's been Elizabeth Taylor; in the 1920s it was Mary Pickford. And these archetypal women are quite often from foreign countries; Greta Garbo from Sweden, the dream woman of the 1930s, is a perfect example. There was another Swedish woman, who arrived in America nearly 150 years ago and, in spite of being modest and self-effacing, took this country by storm. She was a soprano, and her name was Jenny Lind, fondly known as the "Swedish Nightingale." Under the management of P.T. Barnum, she toured the United States from 1850 to '52.

To us, accustomed as we are to the glamour of movie and television stars, it seems odd that this dove-colored creature should have made an impact on the women of her generation. But her fame as an opera singer in Europe had preceded her to America, and her debut in the summer of 1850 at the historic Castle Gardens Theater in New York was a sensation. The house was packed to overflowing, the applause was thunderous.

So it is not surprising that Jenny Lind souvenirs appeared swiftly, everywhere, and women were quick to copy her hairstyle and her clothes, especially her concert dress, a crinoline of almost-olive-green gauze with a wide, straight band of lace from shoulder to shoulder as its only ornament.

But there was no Jenny Lind doll (although there was a paper doll), to the enduring frustration of generations of doll collectors, particularly during the earlier days of this hobby, when hopes ran high, and imaginations were unbounded. The old doll books are full of "Jenny Lind dolls," all of them, I'm afraid, spurious. At a time when unusual china heads were very popular, it was a common fancy to give such heads quite unsubstantiated names: Mary Todd Lincoln, for instance, and the even more unlikely Dolley Madison. One particularly beautiful head with swept-back wings of hair on each side of the face was dubbed the Jenny Lind. These misnomers remain obstinately in use

This china-head doll was given to the Museum of the City of New York in 1935 by Katharine H. Meigs, the daughter of the doll's original owner, Katharine Anna Bryan.

they also have the real thing, documented!" A genuine Jenny Lind doll! I was, of course, excited and made it my business to seek out this paragon among dolls.

Well, of course, it is not a genuine Jenny Lind for there still is no such thing, I'm afraid. This doll has a rare and very lovely china head; it is one of the early brown-haired chinas of a German or Danish porcelain factory. It has a gentle face, serious and dignified, and the brown hair lies in two heavy loops in front of the ears, a little like the style made so popular by Queen Victoria.

This is an uncommon head, but when you do find one, usually it has a porcelain knot of hair at the nape of the neck. This Jenny Lind, however, has no knot. There is no damage, either, that would suggest the knot had broken off. I have seen one other head finished, or rather, unfinished, in this same way. Perhaps one afternoon the workmen were careless, or had imbibed or had even run out of clay. Whatever the reason, the dolls' heads weren't important enough for the imperfect ones to be thrown away.

So how does this rare but anonymous doll become a genuine Jenny Lind? Now the answer to this question is fascinating— and documented, too—so my enthusiastic collector friends were at least partly right. It is the doll's dress that is documented.

to this very day, although there isn't the slightest excuse for them, excepting the caprice of our predecessors.

I had of course heard of these Jenny Lind dolls, and when I joined the staff of the Museum of the City of New York as curator of toys, my collecting friends were jubilant. "Oh, they have such wonderful dolls hidden away," they enthused. "And now you will be able to bring them all to light. Why, they even have a genuine Jenny Lind, not the black-haired china with those swept-back wings. They have one of those as well, but

Amongst the crowds of New Yorkers who thronged to Castle Gardens for that first legendary concert by Jenny Lind was a young lady who had purchased our brown-haired doll that very afternoon. It was to be a birthday gift for a young relative, and the dressing of it had been very much on her mind as she prepared for the concert. Like everyone else, she was overwhelmed by the Swedish Nightingale, and as she lay in bed that night waiting for sleep, with that glorious voice still echoing in her head, it occurred to her that she could dress the doll as Jenny Lind in the famous green gauze concert dress.

She was up early the next morning and off to the department store. There she found, to her amazement, a queue of ladies waiting at the fabric counter. And they were all buying the green gauze fabric, which an astute store buyer had providently laid in stock. There must have been Jenny Linds at all the fashionable evening parties in New York that summer! When this girl finally reached the counter, the green gauze was sold out but, luckily, the store had also stocked it in a narrow scarf width, which of course was perfectly adequate for the doll. It was borne home in triumph, made up with the appropriate lace bertha straight across from shoulder to shoulder and was received by the birthday girl with rapture. This very special doll was treasured in the family until the 1930s, when a descendant presented it to the Museum of the City of New York.

I am sure it had been preserved very carefully within the family, but by the time I was holding it in my hands, in 1961, the dress was in tatters. The crinoline skirt was split in several places; the lining of the bodice and puffed sleeves were shredded; and the lace bertha had disappeared altogether. It was a sorry sight and impossible to exhibit. So it remained for the next 20 years, an embarrassment when, as so often happened, it was enquired about, and also a great disappointment after all my hopes and anticipation. But in the early 1980s, a young lady appeared in my office who changed all this.

Her name was Margaret Molnar; she was a professional fabric conservator trained at the legendary school in Bern, Switzerland. I have sung Margaret's praises in this magazine on other occasions, including the premiere issue, when I described how she helped to discover, and then restore so brilliantly, the wonderful dolls' dresses made in the 1860s by Charles Frederick Worth. But the first doll on which Margaret worked

...the Jenny Lind doll stands before us today dignified and beautiful, looking very much as she must have looked in the summer of 1850...

was our so-called Jenny Lind.

"It's a very simple restoration," she had said offhandedly. "You could really do it yourself, you know!" Modesty comes in all colors. Margaret's processes were intricate and painstaking, and we followed them with awe, for this was our first exposure to professional conservation procedures.

The gauze is a delicate fabric, the warp being a very fine linen thread, while the weft is an even finer woolen one; it needed to be handled with the utmost caution. First, the dress was carefully taken apart, the tattered pieces smoothed out and tacked into place on a backing. Then these pieces were wet-cleaned, a process very different from laundering. Next, the clean tatters and wisps of gauze were arranged and pinned onto a superfine, almost invisible silken net, known by the trade name Crepeline. "Now, I have to mount the gauze," said Margaret, again almost offhandedly. "It will take some weeks, I'm afraid. I hope you're not in a hurry!" We soon found out why, for Margaret sewed with an almost invisible needle and thread, wearing a sort of portable microscope, as you and I would wear reading glasses. A long afternoon's work would produce only an inch or two of sewing. Meanwhile, the bodice lining was wet-cleaned and by some alchemy restored to its former shape.

When the dress was reassembled, it fitted perfectly, and it was crisp and fresh. Armed with engravings of Jenny in her concert gown, we applied to the museum's costume collection and were given enough handmade lace of the proper width, weight and period to reproduce convincingly that so-important bertha. The result is lovely, but unassuming, just as was Jenny Lind herself. This is not a spectacular restoration guaranteed to knock your socks off, as do the restored Worth dresses. But the Jenny Lind doll stands before us today dignified and beautiful, looking very much as she must have looked in the summer of 1850, when her proud little owner saw her for the very first time—and only a day or two after the real Jenny Lind's triumph.

And that (at least for this museum curator emeritus) is a very satisfactory conclusion to what was, as you will surely agree, a very romantic story.

A Few of His Favorite Things

As I move contentedly into my 70s, I am surprised to discover what a vast conglomeration, what an Aladdin's treasury of objects I love in this world—and love with a startling passion. If you are a collector, you may be lucky enough eventually to own some of your Favorite Things, and if you live to a decent old age, as I have, with or without possession, the beloved objects will proliferate.

I am an admitted old sentimentalist, so it is not surprising that, amongst that king's ransom of Favorite Things, there are a few that are particularly close to my heart. This is because in some way, they have played an important, and sometimes even crucial, part in my life. And so it is with the group of dolls depicted on these pages.

When I first came to America in April 1960, it was for a long summer holiday, to be spent in New York City and on Fire Island; I had every intention of returning to England in October of that year. One of the very first things that I did upon my arrival was to make a pilgrimage to the Museum of the City of New York, to its Toy Collection. For 20 years, I had been reading about and dreaming over its treasures, especially its historic dollhouses.

During that spring of 1960, the museum was featuring a new acquisition in a special display located in the entrance hall. It was the Brett Dolls' House, a remarkable structure, built in 1835 by the Reverend Milledoler Brett for his little nieces, in the sail loft of the family's shipping business on the famous South Street. I was fascinated by it, for it was quite unlike the English houses of my acquaintance, and I made an appointment to see

Known as the Raymond doll, this circa-1815, 14-inch mask-face wooden was a gift to the Museum of the City of New York by Sophia L. McDonald, as were all the dolls shown with this article.

125

including Mehitabel Hodges, the famous Salem doll, of whose saga I wrote in this magazine some years ago ("The Saga of the Salem Doll," Winter 1984). It was a large and important gift, but there was no one at that time on the museum's staff qualified to authenticate its treasures. Carlin wanted to know if I would consider a month's consultancy, in which to do so myself.

Well, of course, I was delighted, and accepted with alacrity, and I spent a very happy month indeed. Carlin and I became great friends, and there were indeed many rare treasures to be explored and gloated over. The quality of the gift was superb, although there were several dolls about which I had reservations, one of these being Mehitabel Hodges, whose story didn't fit with her appearance.

Another famous doll whose authenticity I questioned was the one which for some reason was known as the Raymond doll. Purporting to be an English wooden from the early 18th century, this little lady wears a bronze silk dress with an elaborate hem, tightly sashed, and a lace-trimmed net cap. The doll is a wooden with a mask face of molded plaster, a very late English type. And the dress, although made of old fabrics, was quite unconvincing. Very carefully, Carlin and I removed the clothes.

The Raymond doll had lost her legs, but she had the odd, pointed wooden torso that also means a late date. And when I examined her clothing, there was a delicious surprise, for what had passed as her petticoat was a quite stylish muslin dress of about 1815, a round-gown such as might have been worn by a Jane Austen heroine. It has a high waist and the long sleeves so lamented by Mrs. Bennet in Jane Austen's *Pride and Prejudice*, and its skirt is bordered with two tucks and three flounces. The lace-trimmed cap was of the same vintage, and we saw that the ribbons that tied it were quite modern and had been threaded through holes roughly poked through the lace, perhaps by some child.

Turning to the bronze dress, we steamed away the creases that the sash had made and discovered a second delight, for here was a beautiful

These circa-1815 twin papier-mâché Germans above are each eight inches high. Their dresses have high waists and puffed "transitional" sleeves. The paper label inside the petticoat of this circa-1828 German peg wooden, right, reads: "This doll was bought for Aunt Mary Ann Noyce by her father at Boston when she was a child. Presented to me by Grandma after Aunt died 1866."

the assistant director, Carlin Gasteyer, who was in charge of the Toy Collection in the absence of an official curator. I wanted to learn more of this marvel than what was written on its label.

Carlin and I enjoyed an animated discussion of the dollhouse, and a few weeks later she wrote to me with a proposal. The museum's Toy Collection had been offered a lavish gift of dolls by a collector in California, Sophia L. McDonald, who boasted that she only collected rarities. The gift included several legendary dolls,

Regency dress of a slightly later date still, 1818 perhaps, or even 1820. This is not a round-gown, but at the high waist its fullness is gathered to the back on drawstrings. The full sleeves have ruched ruffles, and the hem of the dress has an elaborate border of zircon-blue velvet, applied with a dagged upper outline. What was offered as an indifferent 18th-century example transpired instead to be a spectacular Regency treasure.

Later still was a German peg wooden, a beautiful example with prim painted curls resting on her forehead from a center part. She has a high yellow tuck-comb, and wooden pendant earrings with traces of red paint. This doll had been fashionably dressed in the late 1820s, and her high-waisted dress of printed cotton has a blue-gray honeycomb pattern on a white ground. Its leg-of-mutton sleeves are most carefully set in at the shoulder, and there is a ruffled hem. We lifted this skirt when we photographed her, to show off the hem of the first petticoat, diapered in regular points, a needle-woman's tour-de-force that is difficult enough on a human scale, but a veritable triumph on a small doll. As a last touch, this peg wooden wears, on a chain of steel beads, a contemporary watch, many sizes too big for her, with an enchanting engraved dial.

Amy and Lucinda Lyseth, twin English woodens, 8 1/2 inches high, are dressed alike in the style from the end of the 18th century, when fashion hit a peak of extravagant frivolity.

Twin dolls are always delicious, and Mrs. McDonald's gift included two pairs of twins. The earlier came with their names, Amy and Lucinda Lyseth, and these again were English woodens with molded plaster mask faces and with cloth arms and legs. They had been dressed alike at the very end of the 18th century, when fashion hit a peak of extravagant frivolity that was as brilliant as it was short-lived.

These two young ladies have high-waisted dresses of white embroidered net lined with crimson ribbons. Their hats are made of white linen, eccentrically trimmed, and have their brims turned back with a kind of careless panache typical of that period, and almost impossible to duplicate. The silk linings are shattered, and it would be a simple task to replace them, but I have always resisted this restoration, for these dolls in their present condition are

the perfect embodiment of the dash and verve of the last decade of the 18th century, preserved for us by the fashion plates of Nicolas Heideloff, and very rarely, in three dimension, like this absurd pair of twins.

The second pair are later by as much as 20 or 25 years, and they, too, by extraordinary coincidence, reflect perfectly the mood of their times. Like the Raymond doll, these date from the Regency era, gentle, modest creatures compared to the flamboyant Lyseth sisters. They are early examples of those German dolls with as yet no satisfactory name—Coiffure Papier-Mâché—being so cumbersome, while the old term Milliners Models is meaningless and misleading.

These twins have papier-mâché heads on stiff kid bodies with rigid wooden limbs. Their hair is molded in high cornets with applied side curls of human hair. They wear demure net caps, and their dresses of embroidered net have the tight wrist-length sleeves with shoulder puffs that were a transitional fashion leading up to the huge, leg-of-mutton sleeves of the 1830s. One doll has blue-painted shoes and yellow ribbons, the other yellow-painted shoes and pink ribbons, but otherwise these rare twins are identical and like the Lyseth sisters, are a perfect embodiment of the spirit of their era.

The museum was so pleased with my report that the trustees raised funds to extend my consultancy for a year, during which time I was to review the condition of the whole Toy Collection. I renewed my visa, and by proxy arranged to let my London flat. When the year was up, to my great pleasure and satisfaction, I was offered a permanent place on the museum staff. I became as assistant curator, in charge of the Toy Collection, but I was soon elevated to a full curatorship, a position I was to hold for the next 30 years.

So you see, these innocent-looking little dolls helped to change my life. I haven't seen them in person now for a number of years, but I shall always remember them with much pride and much affection. They are, indeed, very high up on that seemingly endless list of my Favorite Things!

Chinas In My Charge

I n the last issue of *Dolls*, I wrote of a few of my favorite things. Since this has transpired to be a popular article (others are sentimental, it seems, besides myself), I have delved a little further into the memories of those hectic days, when I was a very busy curator at the Museum of the City of New York.

My office there was in a half-underground basement. The carpet was of necessity dark, and my first impression was of such gloominess that I made a bold decision and had the room painted a brilliant fuchsia with white woodwork. The gloom was at once dispelled, and I found, to my pleasure, that I had created an ambience in which both people and objects looked their best (an important consideration when both donors and underwriters were to be received there).

The Decorative Arts Collection had received an important gift of original Duncan Phyfe furniture, and it had included a modern reproduction of a mahogany bureau topped with a glass-fronted bookcase. This was a very handsome piece, but because it was a reproduction it was offered to the curatorial offices and settled into mine.

I was pleased to house this particular piece, because it could be locked and was as secure as the museum display cases upstairs. Thus, some of my favorite things could always be in the office with me, to lend luster to what was an important reception area and, incidentally, to give me daily pleasure. The objects on display in the bookcase were changed every month or so, but they often

The doll at right is the largest and most splendid of the author's favorite china dolls. He is 20 inches high and belonged to John Barry Moore, the father of Iola Moore, who donated the doll to the museum. Opposite page: Young Victoria, right, so named because of her braided-bun coiffure, worn by the young Queen Victoria when she married Prince Albert in 1840, is 17 inches high. She is featured with Yankee Tom, who wears a coat of an interesting, archaic cut, closed high at the throat but left open down the front. He was a gift of Sophia L. McDonald.

included the dolls described here, since I was so very fond of them.

Three of these chinas are of the very desirable early kind with brown painted hair, instead of the later, almost ubiquitous, black. Like so many of their kind, these dolls are all unmarked, but similar ones are known to be the products of illustrious china factories, such as the Royal Porcelain Manufactory of Berlin and the Royal Copenhagen Manufactory. All three dolls date, I believe, from the 1840s, and although they came from three different donors, they have a family resemblance and are very much in harmony with each other.

The serious-faced young lady in the photo on the preceding page is known as a Young Victoria type, and the reason for this appellation is not hard to understand, since this is exactly the braided-bun hairstyle worn by the young Queen Victoria when she was married to her fairytale Prince Albert in 1840. As might be expected, this coiffure became popular all over the world, and although it remained fashionable for a number of years (into the 1850s, in fact), it certainly helps to date this lovely doll. This Young Victoria, with a sawdust-stuffed cloth body, has beautiful china forearms and wears her original printed cotton dress that shows off her smooth, deep shoulders. (She also came with a blue silk dress, which is boxed separately.) She was a gift to the Toy Collection from the legendary collector Grant Keehn.

The boy doll standing beside Victoria came to us with his name. He is called Yankee Tom, and he was part of a wonderful bonanza gift from a neighboring museum, the Cooper-Hewitt Museum, also on Fifth Avenue in New York City. Their textile department had, through the years, accumulated a number of fine dolls, and their curator felt that they would be of more value in a toy collection. Needless to say, we accepted this generous gift with surprise and much pleasure. Yankee Tom quickly became a great favorite of mine, and he was often to be found in the display case in the fuchsia-colored office. He is quite a serious little fellow. His body is homemade, and, unfortunately, he came to us with one kid hand. His clothes, which are also homemade, are very endearing. He wears a fine lawn shirt with a black silk ribbon cravat, and his blue cashmere coat contrasts with his nankeen "trowsers." This coat is of an interesting, archaic cut, closed high at the throat but left open down the front, although it sports, as decoration, a double row of mother-of-pearl buttons.

The largest and most splendid of my favorite china dolls is the brown-haired boy on the opening page of this story. Named Willie, he dates from about 1845, and his glorious unmarked, pink-tinted head is possibly by

Konigliche Porzellan Manufaktur. His features are sensitively modeled under his "windblown" hair, and he has a most fascinating, enigmatic expression. He has a homemade cloth body with stitched toes and kid-leather arms.

His costume is fascinating, too. He wears formal, black-and-gray striped trousers and a green corded silk vest. But instead of the waisted, skirted coat one would expect from this period, he wears instead a figured cotton *banyon*, which was worn informally at home, just as a smoking jacket or dressing jacket would be worn at later dates. His tall "beaver" hat is, of course, outdoor wear and implies the coats and greatcoats, cloaks and canes that he doubtless possessed at one time, and which are now, alas, missing.

However, as with all rare old dolls, we must be humbly grateful for what has survived to us. The beaver hat invites us to dream of missing sartorial splendors, and the *banyon* is an uncommon enough survivor in real life, and almost unheard-of among dolls. It is interesting to note that this doll belonged, not to a little girl, but to a boy, John Barry Moore, born in 1851. The doll seems at least a few years earlier, so perhaps John Barry inherited it?

The black-haired china doll on the left in the photo on the opposite page is somewhat later than the brown-haired chinas we have already looked at. Dating from the early 1850s, she is a lovely example, with deep shoulders, white kid arms with stitched, separate fingers, and a simple but most elegant coiffure. From a center parting, her hair falls smoothly in 12 pendant curls to her shoulders. According to the marking on her commercially made cloth body, she originally cost $1.25, a good deal to pay for a doll in those days.

She came to us with only a straw bonnet and rose-pink kid shoes. But the museum has amassed over the years what could truthfully be called a costume collection in miniature, and I had the pleasure of finding suitable underclothes for this doll, besides the neat blue-and-white cotton print dress and the fancy printed cotton apron, both of the proper period, that she wears in the photograph. She was the gift of Jane Watson Crane, who also gave to the museum one of its more major treasures, the richly furnished Elder Dolls' House, which is of approximately the same date as this doll.

The remaining two dolls in this picture are new to me, for they were accepted into the collection after I had left. However, they are enchanting and would certainly have joined that exclusive little gathering of my favorite china dolls. They are of a similar date to the Crane doll just described and they all make a harmonious group. They might even be by the same manufacturer, although there

These three circa-1850 chinas are later examples than the other three shown with the article. The 20-1/2-inch doll at far left wears a period dress found for her by the author, as she was donated by Jane Watson Crane with only a bonnet and shoes. Although the other two chinas were donated to the museum after the author left (by Darcy B., Harriet R.T. and Tanya T. Kelley, granddaughters of the original owner, Harriet Richards Tweedy Wildman), they are enchanting enough to have joined his exclusive gathering of favorite china dolls.

is, of course, no way of telling. But the quality of the china, the coloring, and above all, the superb modeling, all suggest a common origin.

The little boy sitting up in bed is beguilingly thoughtful, and he has tousled, brush-marked hair. He was given to the museum together with the older doll in the red cloak, who was named Florence by the original owner. Florence has a magnificent head; her high forehead and curiously high crown are complemented by her long neck

and deep, sloping shoulders. These physical attributes make her hairstyle, which is, in fact, so similar to that of the doll in the blue dress, at once more striking and more fashionable. Here the pendant curls are much longer, and they are heavier and more crisply modeled. The hairstyle is undercut, too, in a manner rarely attempted by the craftspeople who modeled these heads, as, of course, they were more difficult to cast, having a higher proportion of failure. But the result is very lovely.

I said goodbye to these beloved dolls over six years ago, and although I have many other favorite dolls around me, and indeed, many other favorite things of all kinds, these china dolls remain very dear to my heart. They greatly enriched those kaleidoscopic days in that fuchsia-colored office, and I shall always remember them very fondly. And it is now my great pleasure to share them with my readers.

A Story of
Suitable Sentiments

A FAMILY'S REVERED 18TH-CENTURY WOODEN IS NOW
A MUSEUM'S DOCUMENTED TREASURE

Doll collectors come from all walks of life, so it is not surprising that dolls are valued for many different qualities. To the artistic, visually-oriented collectors, the beauty of the doll is paramount; to the sentimental ones, the emotional appeal takes precedence. Rarity, distinguished provenance, even mere age, can be the desirable quality, to the right collector. For a museum collection, all of these attributes can be important, but a museum, especially a history museum, will value yet another aspect of a doll, which perhaps may not appeal, or even occur, to most collectors. The attribute I speak of is continuity or, as defined by Webster's, "an uninterrupted connection." All dolls, indeed all surviving artifacts from the past, come with continuity, but for the most part, it has been lost quite early on the way. This is a great pity, but one rejoices greatly when some treasure from the past does indeed, by good fortune, come down to us with all its continuity.

I remember a house in Pennsylvania where I was once invited to tea. It was a farmhouse, built of stone, early in the 18th century, when it was a simple four-room structure. As the family grew and prospered, each generation added on a piece to the old house, straight out, on either side: a late-18th-century stone extension, much grander than the first house; then a Federal wing, wooden clapboard with wonderful paneling inside; then a pretty gingerbread extension with a verandah; and finally, a big 20th-century

The 22-inch-high circa-1805 wooden shown at right belonged to two different girls named Mary King during the course of her lifetime. Her clothing, including the professionally made straw poke bonnet is dated circa 1844. She was a gift to the Museum of the City of New York by the second Mary King, later known as Dr. Mary Murray Lowden. Mary King wears a rather eclectic outfit. The chemise, pantalets, silk stockings, tan-and-blue printed cotton dress, net apron and kerchief are circa 1844, and were probably made by the first Mary King. Later additions were the flame-stitched purse (said to be made by the second Mary King) and the moccasins made on a Native American reservation in Canada.

piece, very "modern," with a swimming pool. Walking through that house was like walking through time! I know of a German bisque doll, too, which is still loved and cherished in the family that has always owned her. The original 1890 wardrobe, very carefully preserved, has been complemented by each generation, with new, fashionable clothes. Her continuity, the unbroken story of her progress through 100 years within the same family, is a happy story, and I could only wish for many others. What could our old dolls tell us, if only their continuity had not been destroyed? But I'm afraid it nearly always is.

Dolls, more than most antiques, are objects haunted by love, and their progress through the years and then through the centuries, their ups and downs as they pass perhaps from a loving first owner to a careless second one, their solitary sojourns in neglect—and even in disgrace—in attics and basements, their rescues, their subsequent collectors, each one valuing them differently—all this makes fascinating reading, in the very few instances where such documentation of continuity is preserved.

I am sorry that I have no photographs of the German bisque doll to offer, but the subject of this article, an 18th-century English wooden doll called Mary King, is a similar treasure. True, her real story extends over no more than two generations. After that, for more than 100 years she sat calmly in the bosom of her family, revered and respected, until the day when she was given to the Toy Collection of the Museum of the City of New York. But her story is no less enchanting for being so brief.

Mary King is a classic 18th-century English wooden, a late example but a very fine one. "She's a beauty!" visiting collectors used to say to me when I offered Mary King for their inspection. "But what a pity she's been redressed. Why don't you find her some proper clothes?" they would inevitably ask. Let me now explain why.

The doll was brought to New York from Holland in 1805 by Joseph King for his little daughter, Mary. She doubtless came with "proper clothes," but whether she was a quaint, old-fashioned doll from the 1780s or '90s, dressed in a corset and panniers, or whether she was

> ...we must remember that the 1840s were a particularly sentimental decade, when the quaintness of the re-dressed old doll would have been much appreciated.

bought new, the last of her line, and wearing a high-waisted "Jane Austen" dress, we shall never know.

We do know that Mary King treasured her, and kept her safe after she grew up. Apparently Mary didn't marry, but her sister did, and Mary was godmother to her niece, who was named after her. When Mary King Murray was ten years old, in the early 1840s, her aunt Mary decided to give her the treasured old doll.

I can imagine her sitting, sewing the new dolls' clothes—the finely stitched petticoat and the pretty cotton print dress—before giving the doll to her niece. The doll was given a new wig, with fashionable corkscrew curls, and a straw bonnet to wear over her cap—a bonnet so elaborate that I am sure it was made especially by Mary King's milliner.

Mary King Murray must have been enraptured with her present—we must remember that the 1840s were a particularly sentimental decade, when the quaintness of the re-dressed old doll would have been much appreciated. At any rate, Mary King Murray kept her doll very carefully, and when she arrived in the museum, all her clothing was in perfect condition.

A story has been passed down to us that Mary King taught her niece embroidery and needlepoint, and the doll's little flame-stitched purse is evidence of the child's efforts. It is interesting that this archaic stitch was chosen, suiting the doll so very well, and bridging the gap between the generations.

At one point, the child was taken on holiday to Canada and, not surprisingly, her doll accompanied her. She visited a Native American reservation, where a tiny pair of moccasins was made for the doll, and it is easy to imagine the Native-American women's reactions to the sober, well-behaved child with her old-fashioned treasure. The doll has worn this incongruous footwear ever since.

Purist collectors may still think that the doll Mary King is disfigured, and wish her 1840 clothes away. But for me, this doll is the stuff of history, the very substance of imagination and magic. I could wish that hundreds of other, equally fascinating dolls had come down to us, like Mary King, with their histories, their continuities, safely intact.

The Bru Family that Nearly Wasn't

A CAUTIONARY TALE FROM THE DAYS WHEN DOLLS WERE TOO EASILY DISCARDED

This is a tale from the dark ages of doll collecting, and I tell it here partly because it has a happy ending—and I love happy endings! And then, too, the protagonists, a little family of early Bru child dolls, are so utterly enchanting that I long to share them with my readers. But there is another reason for the telling of this little story from the dark ages, and that is to heed it as a tale of caution. I know that amongst my readership there are a number of curators of small local museums and historical societies who are at this time facing much the same crisis as the museum in my story was facing. Operating costs mount alarmingly, funds are cut back, storage is a nightmare, and the weeding of the accumulation of artifacts becomes of paramount importance.

I came to America from England in 1960 and joined the permanent staff of the Museum of the City of New York only a few years later. I was treated from the first with a sort of amused tolerance, which quickly changed to affection, but was very slow in changing to respect. Due to my serious interest in the dolls and toys of other days, I was thought to be verging on lunacy. At that time, old playthings were almost invisible in the world of antiques. Only the earliest and rarest examples ever appeared in auction houses; the collectors' clubs were in their infancy; and I saw in a Madison Avenue shop window a glorious little Jumeau bébé of the finest quality, priced quite a long way below a hundred dollars!

In the museum context, the old playthings were thought of as, at best, odd flowers to pop into the buttonhole of an exhibition to lend a little color or an added fillip. "Well, you don't need proper storage," said a decorative-arts curator one day when we were lamenting the paucity of space. "After all, your collections are just stuff! It isn't as if they were important!"

There certainly was no proper storage for the Toy Collection, when I first went to work for the museum. It was tucked away in nooks and corners, all over the building, and as there were usually no locks to its cupboards and drawers, priceless treasures were constantly exposed to vandalism and theft. The wonderful dolls were, when I first saw them, piled precariously on open shelves under the roof, over a cement

play of the museum's dolls was organized. This neglected treasury was brought into the spotlight. Unfortunately, the Education Department was desperately in need of funds, as there were hundreds of neglected, dirty dolls that had to be tended to, and so, very quietly, a series of sales of supposedly superfluous dolls and toys took place.

Now, I must hasten to say that this is an established museum practice, and one without which a growing museum cannot survive for very long. What was so tragic in the case of the Toy Collection was that the Education Department personnel in charge at that time had no concept of the importance or the value of the dolls and toys in their care. They had no idea of what they were disposing. For the next few years, I found myself searching for what I thought

These two ten-inch Bru bébé twins were, luckily, reunited by the author, after one twin was lost in the museum for years. The circa-1875 dolls have bisque swivel heads on leather bodies carrying paper labels that read: "Bébé Breveté SGDG Paris." Each wears a white tucked petticoat and nightdress with a tucked bib front, and a lace cap. They, along with their brother, shown on the preceding page, and another set of twins sold in the 1950s, were a gift to the Museum of the City of New York by George Chapman.

floor. Many were thick with dust, and many were broken. "Well, they were for many years in the charge of the Education Department," I was told. "And no one there seems to have thought much of them."

Well, one wishes that this had always been so and that they had simply left them all lying there for me to find and restore later. But in the mid 1950s, a national doll convention was held in New York City, and to coincide with it, a dis-

were treasures in the museum's collection, only to discover from the registrar that they had been sold in the 1950s weeding.

One of my early discoveries was the little family of Brus illustrated here. I found one of the twins, and their older brother in his green velvet jacket, on one of the dusty piles in the museum's attic. I checked the accession cards for the dolls and found that the dolls had been part of a Bru family, given as a gift to the museum in 1941. The accession cards had been updated in the late 1950s, and the boy's card bore this cryptic sentence: "Brother to identical twins, 41.359.3 & 5, and to discarded 41.359.2 & 4." Discarded! Two members of a rare little Bru family discarded! Why?

The correspondence files produced a clue. The dolls had been sold, with several others, to a reputable dealer in quite proper circumstances in the '50s. I was the only person who mourned their parting. However, a curious fact emerged from the correspondence. "I would have liked to take the twins," wrote the dealer, "But since one of them is lost, I really don't want just the other one." So now I had a mystery on my hands: where was the missing twin, and how on earth was it lost? When I reported the missing doll to the laconic registrar, a gentleman who also considered the Toy Collection to be just so much stuff, I was told, "Oh, don't worry, the other one must be about, somewhere!" As the years went by, however, the twin didn't show up, and I worried more and more about this lost Bru treasure.

Meanwhile, the piles of dusty dolls were gradually being cleaned, and repaired and stored properly, and amongst them, I found the little Bru girl shown above. She was a much later gift, and an amusing note on her card, dating from the 1950s debacle, reads "Unmarked Bru, one finger broken, value $100.00." But then, the 1950s were a long time ago, weren't they? I stood her with the two other Brus, and they liked each other at once. So, the little girl joined the Bru family, perhaps as a distant cousin, and the sec-

Although this 12-inch unmarked Bru was a later gift to the museum than the others, the author added her to the family as he felt she was, perhaps, a distant cousin. (Gift of Beatrice Maude)

ond twin remained missing.

It was not until the mid 1970s that this mystery was solved. At that time, the crowded Education Department was expanded. Some structural alterations necessitated a thorough turnout, and some antiquated office furniture was replaced. And it was at the back of a deep desk drawer, buried under piles of old letters, that I found the missing twin!

"Oh, so that's the one you were looking for!" said a long-time volunteer. "Oh, I can remember how this came about," she offered. It seems that there had once been a cherubic-looking typist in the Education Department, long since gone on her way, and she had been given a lavish office party to celebrate her 21st birthday. Someone fancied a resemblance between the typist and the Bru twin, and it had been presented to her, seated in a rosette of tissue paper, on the big pink birthday cake! She was delighted, and for quite a while after that, the doll sat on her desk. No one noticed when it eventually disappeared into the drawer. And so, fortunately, it survived the 1950s weeding (which, in my mind, will always be the 1950s holocaust!).

Of course, all this happened in the Toy Collection's dark ages. Today, there is a whole wing of one floor of the building given over to the collection, which is stored with proper orderliness and security. There will never be those desolate, dusty heaps of neglected treasures, ever again. The survivors of the little Bru family are known and admired by doll collectors all over the world, and this is just as it should be.

But, as I said before, I am sure there still exist many small, struggling museums and rural historical societies that have dusty storerooms and plethoras of artifacts, useless to the museums' declared purpose and taking up valuable space. If so, and their curators are reading this article, I do advise them to move very cautiously indeed.

For this story of the missing Bru, in the end, is a cautionary tale, despite its happy ending!

Blessedly Untouched,
Except by Time

A REFLECTION ON THE PRECARIOUS SURVIVAL OF MOST OLD DOLLS' HOUSES

Here are two little dolls' houses from the Wenham Museum, in Wenham, Massachusetts: both modest little structures, with none of the historical importance of, for instance, the Brett House in the Museum of the City of New York, or the glitter and glamour of Colleen Moore's Fairy Castle in Chicago's Museum of Science and Industry. So why am I so delighted with them, and feel so privileged to present them here? And why does my heart sing when I look at them?

"We all destroy the things we love—" I can't remember at the moment the precise quotation, but it always comes to mind if I think of the fate of most old dolls' houses when they come on the market. Today, it has become almost impossible to locate an old dolls' house that is in precisely the same condition in which it was left by its original owner.

This modest dolls' house with only four rooms, once owned by the Haviland family, is dated 1891. The house has no facade; instead, a curtain rod across the front perhaps held a curtain or pair of curtains. The dining room, left, has a classical frieze with acanthus leaves; the entire ceiling has been papered. Unfortunately, no table settings have survived.

The ranks of passionate dolls' house collectors have swollen immeasurably in the past 30 years, and dealers were quick to realize even before then that much, oh much, more profit could be gained by taking an old dolls' house apart, selling its dolls and its furniture, its furnishings and accessories all separately, and finally offering the house itself for sale, an empty shell. As Vivien Greene, in reference to such a devastated dolls' house, commented sadly, "*toute passe, toute casse, toute lasse.*" (Everything fades away, everything breaks, everything becomes tiresome.)

There are, of course, the dwindling, precious few houses still treasured by their original families—and how one longs for them to remain there! And then, blessedly, there are the lucky houses that were bequeathed in safer days to museums. However one may deplore their long sojourns in storage, with their furnishings stacked and packed away, at least they have been preserved intact, immune from predatory fingers. Such are my two Wenham treasures.

Let us look first at the larger of the two. It is a modest dolls' house, with only four rooms, two up and two down, and never a thought of a staircase. Nevertheless, the proportions are most elegant, and so is the roofline, with its pagoda curves. There is no facade—odd for such a refined house—but a curtain rod across the entire front implies a decorative curtain, or a pair of curtains, perhaps.

There is almost no documentation, but we do know that this house belonged to the Haviland family (yes, the "porcelain" Havilands!). The crimson and gold pediment bears, amidst leafy flourishes, the initials "M. H. P." and the date, 1891; but for this evidence, I should have dated this structure some 20 years earlier. It is always possible for a house to have been handed down and renovated for its new young owner, and this may have happened here—in which case, of course, the original facade may have already been lost.

However it comes about, this house is most beautifully finished. Silver-gilt moldings enrich the edges of the partitions, the three main rooms have elaborate cornices, while the drawing room, or parlor, can boast both skirtings and a most splendid frieze. Above the gentle, biscuit-colored walls, this frieze is a daring extravaganza, for on a black background, a border of giant field flowers sprawls around the room in a monochrome of shaded gold. This bold decoration is repeated on the ceiling itself, and is balanced by a carpet with a similar, but more subdued, pattern. It is a startling but successful decor, worthy of a great designer—even of Cecil Beaton himself. The furnishings are good 1890 pieces, with some very nice gilt-metal accessories, and the total effect is warm and inviting.

The bedroom has a delicious floral wallpaper with a sky-blue ground, and it has another spectacular cornice. The same carpet looks different here, in this gentler ambiance. The furniture is sober and well chosen, and again, there are several very nice gilt-metal pieces—the chandelier, the pedestal birdcage, the sewing table and the sewing machine. The cardboard trunk is a candybox and may be older than the rest, while the telephone is

The parlor boasts an extravagant frieze, skirtings and a subdued carpet that balances the dramatic design of the frieze—giant field flowers against a black background. The furnishings are circa 1890.

obviously later, as is the oil heater—just like the one put in my bedroom on cold winter nights when I as a child in London! This is in its sum a very pretty room, a room in which one would wake up refreshed and happy.

The dining room, on the other hand, is a most serious chamber—no frivolities here! The entire ceiling has been richly and darkly papered. There is a classical frieze with acanthus leaves, its crimson and gold pomp echoed by the furniture, with its crimson plush and its air of forbidding formality. No table settings seem to have survived, which is a pity, for a white damask cloth and colored table china would have lightened this room and made it more inviting.

And so we come to the kitchen, and here we find the prettiest floor covering in the house. The furnishings here are what one might expect, from the stolid cast-iron stove to the serviceable pots and pans. The milk can is as appropriate as the butter churn is a surprise, and the very handsome wall telephone is of course another anachronism. There are two very nice pets, a china cat sitting on a chair (its twin is in one of my own dolls' houses) and a tiny bronze dog, which is playing with an equally tiny bronze piccanniny—oddly enough, the only inhabitant of this very desirable residence.

There are odd and charming discrepancies—the vases of flowers on the floor, for instance, and the extra clock beside them. This is reassuring, implying as it does that everything belonging to the house is put out for us to see. We step back after this close inspection to survey the house in its entirety and again, I for one am enchanted. Undisturbed and unmolested, this little house is brimming with character, a microcosm of the modes and manners of its own time and place.

The second house from Wenham is sadly shabby, but I must warn you, it is one of my favorite dolls' houses. Looked at with a calculating or avaricious eye, it is unprepossessing enough, and I can imagine many a dealer tossing it without ceremony into the trash. But look at it again, with me, and with sympathy and understanding.

This one-room house is from the 1830s, and it belonged to a Miss Annie Bigelow Lawrence—that is all we know about it. Very small, only 7¾ inches wide and less than eleven inches to the peak of the roof, it is nonetheless well made, with four inset windows and its roof supported on half-round pilasters. It is nicely proportioned too, so that it seems bigger than it really is.

It is covered and indeed decorated, both outside and in, entirely with papers, and it is the decaying of these papers that make this little house so pitifully shabby. Imagination is needed here and memory, too, for at the finishing schools for young ladies, both in England and New England, decorative paperwork was one of the accomplishments taught. While the ornamentation of this little house is clumsy enough to be the work of Miss Annie at a tender age, it is easy to imagine her embarking on this project in emulation of the work of an older sister.

Clumsy, perhaps, but very pretty it must have been when it was new. The exterior was all blue-gray, the windows and the roof line carefully bordered in cream. Inside, Miss Annie made a dado of the same blue-gray paper, and to place above her fireplace she found, perhaps from a cigarbox, a splendid crowned Irish harp in a garland of shamrocks, all in gold on a velvety black ground.

Then, taking great pains, she made a border of black paper, with an applied pattern of alternating circles and diamonds, in pink and blue. This border is applied both as a cornice and as a chair-rail, and it outlines the windows with careful neatness. Unless you have attempted this sort of decoration in a small dolls' house, you may be

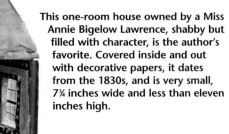

This one-room house owned by a Miss Annie Bigelow Lawrence, shabby but filled with character, is the author's favorite. Covered inside and out with decorative papers, it dates from the 1830s, and is very small, 7¾ inches wide and less than eleven inches high.

unaware of the patience and neatness necessary—and in ratio to a lack of experience and skill. To my mind, this little dolls' house is a triumph of patience and perseverance.

There is a charming wall-to-wall cloth carpet, embroidered in chain stitch, there is a black-and-gold tin ducks'-nest grate, and four quite ravishing flower pictures decorate the fireplace wall. The few furnishings are sadly out of scale, and, I suspect, of a slightly later date and therefore not quite original—I hope so. They are very desirable pieces, of about 1850: a table, two chairs and a pedestal sidetable of American painted tin (how a dealer would snap them up!) and a second pedestal table of painted pewter that is earlier. There are absurd, white shaggy dogs of an unidentifiable breed to enliven the interior—and this is all.

Ah, but cast your mind back! Try to imagine this little house around 1830 with its papers all fresh and neat, the exterior sound and respectable, the borders twinkling pink and blue. Imagine the fragile, pretty, rose-colored furniture with its sabre-legged chairs, so available at that date, and in the right size. And imagine the peg-wooden dolls in their crisp, print dresses and their poke bonnets. For this is all there, just behind the shabbiness.

Splendid houses of this period still stand some chance of being preserved, both by donation to museums and even, today, in the right auction rooms. But a simple, homely, battered little thing like Miss Annie's house—I don't think it would stand a chance.

I suppose I am a sentimental old man, but I was thrilled, years ago, to discover Miss Annie's house, standing unobtrusively—and safely—in a glass case in the Wenham Museum. It set me off, dreaming and conjecturing about little Miss Annie—how proud she must have been, way back in the 1830s, when her little house was finished! And there it is, all these years later, just as shabby but still as safe, if I may coin a phrase, as houses!

And as Shakespeare so aptly said, "So shines a good deed, in a naughty world."

Well-Loved Woodens

A FOND LOOK AT THREE VENERABLE OLD DARLINGS FROM THE WENHAM MUSEUM

It is always a pleasure for me to write about my favorite things, and one of the dolls here has been a firm favorite of mine since I first discovered her, some 30-odd years ago. Today we will again visit the rich collection of dolls at Wenham Museum in Massachusetts and look at three old wooden darlings, all from the 18th century.

One is my favorite, but the two others I have chosen because they have, like the objects that I chose for previous articles, a message and a moral. Both are most interesting and both have their own peculiar style of beauty. And I believe that neither of them would have survived for long in their original condition in the hands of dealers—at least not in the recent unenlightened past, when they first saw the light of 20th-century day.

The first of these 18th-century darlings, a late one, has been very much loved and played with—that we can see at first glance. I have a little collection of old children's books pertaining to dolls, many of them written in the form of dolls' diaries. One of them, the story of a family doll from the 18th century, ends with the doll being fetched down from the attic by the two little boys of the house, and set up as an Aunt Sally [Editor's note: the name given to an effigy of a woman smoking a pipe set up as an amusement attraction at English fairs for patrons to throw missiles at], for them to throw balls at. The doll is perfectly happy and philosophical about this dismaying circumstance. "It is good to be loved and wanted," says the doll in its diary.

"And to be sure, an Aunt Sally is just as useful as any other sort of doll."

I trust that no such alarming fate befell this first doll of ours, although she is known as "the General's doll." But she has certainly been loved almost to death, and she was cared for enough for her head to have been cut off and salvaged, and mounted on a homemade rag body for the pleasure of the next few

Known as the General's doll, shown above and right, the head of this much-loved and played-with wooden from the late 18th century was salvaged and placed on a rag doll body.

This 18th-century wooden attired in a 19th-century calico dress is in pristine condition. No cracks or chips can be seen in her paint, with the possible exception of her smile, which may have been deliberately scraped by a previous young owner.

beautiful. They are sturdy enough to be loved and played with by children for many years—the wear and tear seems to improve them." Bravo, E.J.! This is exactly the beauty that I find in the General's doll—and very rare it is.

The second doll from Wenham is a handsome creature. Again, this is a late-18th-century wooden, and she has a most unusual and enchanting smile, caused, I suspect, by the deliberate scraping of the paint on her lips by some previous little owner. Otherwise, the paint is in amazingly pristine condition—not a chip or even a crack to be seen.

The whole doll is immaculate, and this is remarkable, since she was redressed, very beautifully and precisely, in the mid 19th century. Her brown calico dress fits her perfectly, and very neat and proper it is, with its gathered bodice, its pantalettes, and its discreet lace trim. The wig, I suspect, may be the original one but re-dressed in curls in the manner of the mid-19th century.

Great pains were taken, that is obvious—and then, apparently, this family treasure was not played with again! We know of many instances where dolls were special, kept carefully aside by Mama, and only brought out on rare occasions to be played with, and sometimes only looked at, under Mama's close supervision. I suspect that is what has happened here, and it is the reason for the perfect condition of this family doll, with her layers of love.

And now, with great pleasure, I turn to my own special doll, my own old favorite.

I saw this doll early in the 1960s when she was on exhibit at the Essex Institute in Salem, Massachusetts. I promptly fell in love with her, coveted her, dreamed about her for years. The more I found out about her, the more attractive she became, for she is well documented, and this documentation contains a fascinating discrepancy.

To quote the accession card: "She belonged to

generations of children. I can imagine the repainting and re-dressing and rewigging that would go on were she to come onto the market. And I must say that I am very glad that she is safe at Wenham. She has a powerful presence, this relic of perhaps generations of affection. It is so easy, in our world of collectors, to forget the children for whom our beloved dolls were originally intended, but here, as we encounter this direct, blue gaze, the ghosts of those children come very close to us.

I must note in this context that in his book on dollmaking (*Dollmaking*, Workman Publishing, 1987) the artist E.J. Taylor, giving simple patterns for three classic homemade rag dolls, says: "I don't dress these dolls up, and I don't worry if the measurements are not exact. I find that simplicity of their flat silhouettes very

Susanna Holyoke, daughter of Dr. Edward Augustus Holyoke. In 1795, Susanna went to a ball at the Assembly Hall, Salem, accompanied by her maid. Returning home, the maid dressed this doll in exact imitation of one of the elegantly dressed ladies she saw at the ball. A portrait of Mrs. Nathaniel Bowditch."

As Wenham Museum curator Diane Buck has pointed out, this story does not explain why the dress is considerably earlier than 1795. And yet, this costume is undoubtedly original—indeed, much of the magic of this doll lies not only in the stylishness of her costume, but also very much in her superb original condition. The old splint box, surely of German origin, in which she has survived safely for so long, may indeed be the box in which she was sent from England, all those long years ago. Sometime, quite early on, the box was carefully covered with a scrap

This well-preserved and well-documented doll from 1795, the author's favorite of the three woodens, is the subject of a curious discrepancy: her dress, although original, is of a style 20 years older. The old splint box in which she lies, possibly of German origin, is covered with an 18th-century scenic wallpaper.

of wallpaper—and a very handsome wallpaper it is, a scenic extravaganza carried out in *grisaille*, undoubtedly 18th century—and this in itself indicates that the doll may already have become a family treasure, before that century was over.

There remains the puzzle of the 1770-style dress worn at the 1795 ball. While we know that the fashions are dated by their presence in London or Paris, and the former colonies would have certainly been years behind the times, Salem was nevertheless a major city and a dress 20-odd years out of date would surely be noticeable!

Well, might this not be the answer? Perhaps Mrs. Nathaniel Bowditch was an elderly lady, firmly wearing the old-fashioned clothes that she was accustomed to, like the old countess in The Queen of Spades. She might have been a local eccentric, a figure of fun, and that might be why the maid chose to dress the doll for the child in what would have been a quaint, old-fashioned style. (And was it Susanna the child who went to the ball or was it her mother, also a Susanna?)

This is the pretty story I have concocted to explain the out-of-style dress, and I long that it may be true. But of course, it may also be the case, as it so often is, that family tradition mixes up the dates, and the ball took place earlier. A little professional research could perhaps illuminate this puzzle, as it did when the Colemans looked into the mystery of Mehitabel Hodges, another famous Salem doll ("The Saga of the Salem Doll," Winter 1984).

I hope my readers may derive as much pleasure from my three old darlings as I have had in writing about them. And we must all be grateful to the Wenham Museum, which takes care to preserve so very carefully its many treasures but also has the wisdom to leave them well alone!

Listing of *Dolls* Magazine Articles
by John Darcy Noble

Following is a complete chronological list of the articles written by John Darcy Noble and published in *Dolls* magazine. The articles that appear in this book are indicated by an asterisk.

45